Question Based Bible Study Guide

Nehemiah

Good Questions Have Small Groups Talking

By Josh Hunt

© Copyright 2018 Josh Hunt
josh@joshhunt.com

If you enjoy this, you might check out the hundreds of lessons available at a low subscription price at http://mybiblestudylessons.com/

All scripture quotations, unless otherwise indicated, are taken from the Holy Bible, New International Version®, NIV®. Copyright ©1973, 1978, 1984, 2011 by Biblica, Inc.™ Used by permission of Zondervan. All rights reserved worldwide. www.zondervan.com The "NIV" and "New International Version" are trademarks registered in the United States Patent and Trademark Office by Biblica, Inc.™

Scripture quotations marked (TLB) are taken from The Living Bible copyright © 1971. Used by permission of Tyndale House Publishers, Inc., Carol Stream, Illinois 60188. All rights reserved.

Scripture quotations marked (NLT) are taken from the Holy Bible, New Living Translation, copyright ©1996, 2004, 2007, 2013 by Tyndale House Foundation. Used by permission of Tyndale House Publishers, Inc., Carol Stream, Illinois 60188. All rights reserved.

Scripture quotations from THE MESSAGE. Copyright © by Eugene H. Peterson 1993, 1994, 1995, 1996, 2000, 2001, 2002. Used by permission of Tyndale House Publishers, Inc.

Scripture quotations are from The Holy Bible, English Standard Version® (ESV®), copyright © 2001 by Crossway, a publishing ministry of Good News Publishers. Used by permission. All rights reserved."

Scripture quotations marked HCSB®, are taken from the Holman Christian Standard Bible®, Copyright © 1999, 2000, 2002, 2003, 2009 by Holman Bible Publishers. Used by permission. HCSB® is a federally registered trademark of Holman Bible Publishers.

Contents

Nehemiah: Building a Life of Service

Lesson #1: Pray

Nehemiah 1.1 - 11

OPEN

Share your name and… have you ever built anything?
What have you built

DIG

1. **Today, we begin a study on Nehemiah. Today, we will explore Nehemiah's prayer. I believe if we learn from and follow Nehemiah's example, we will all see dramatic improvement in our prayer lives. And, as our prayer life improves, our whole life will improve. To get us started, let's set the context. What do you know about the life and times and story of Nehemiah?**

   When Solomon died, there was a split in the nations military ranks. Israel became a divided kingdom: Ten tribes migrated to the north and settled in Samaria; the other two went south and settled in Jerusalem and the surrounding areas. The northern tribes during this period of division and civil war are called Israel and the southern group, Judah.

   Just as the lowest ebb in American history was when we took up arms against each other in our Civil War, so it was with this north-south split in Jewish history. They reached their darkest hour nationally, not when they were attacked from without but when they were attacked from within, and the walls of their spiritual heritage began to crumble. During this time of division, all hell literally broke loose. Chaotic conditions prevailed.

God judged Israel when the Assyrians invaded in 722 B.C. Those ten tribes were finished; the Northern Kingdom ceased to exist. But some of the people from the north fled to the south to escape Assyrian control.

The land of Judah remained a Jewish nation for more than three hundred years. However, in 2 586 B.C. Babylon's King Nebuchadnezzar invaded Jerusalem (and all Judah) and took the people captive. This began what is called "the Babylonian Captivity." The biblical account in Chronicles 36:18-19 records the end of Judah's history and the beginning of the Babylonian Captivity.

And all the articles of the house of God, great and small, and the treasures of the house of the Lord, and the treasures of the king and of his officers, he [Nebuchadnezzar, the king of Babylon] brought them all to Babylon. Then they burned the house of God, and broke down the wall of Jerusalem and burned all its fortified buildings with fire, and destroyed all its valuable articles.

They burned the house of God, the temple, and they broke down the protective wall around the city. (Take special note of the words "house of God" and "the wall," for we want to deal with what they mean a bit later.) All the fortified buildings were destroyed with fire as were the valuable articles in the temple.

After the Babylonian takeover, Jerusalem was totally leveled! The magnificent place where God's glory was once displayed was destroyed. The wall lay in ruins, and wild dogs fed upon any edible remains. The armies of Babylon marched back home with all the treasures of Judah.

Psalm 137 was written during this dismal time. The psalmist cried out, "How can we sing the Lords song in a foreign land?" (v. 4). Babylon had come and taken away the Israeli captives. Their song was ended. Second Chronicles 36:20 adds a final word:

And those who had escaped from the sword he carried away to Babylon; and they were servants to him and to his sons until the rule of the kingdom of Persia.

That's important. Those Jews who lived through this siege of Jerusalem were bound together, chained like slaves, and sent to Babylon, a trek of more than eight hundred miles. And under Nebuchadnezzar and his wicked son, the Jews lived as they had centuries before in Egypt, as slaves to a foreign power.

But God didn't forget them. He had a purpose and a plan. Notice how verse 20 concludes: " . . . until the rule of the kingdom of Persia." Here's what happened. There was a king named Cyrus who ruled Persia and another king, Darius, who ruled the neighboring Medes. The two nations were allies, but since the Persian force was the larger of the two, the two countries were often called simply "the kingdom of Persia." The Medes and the Persians invaded Babylon and overthrew it, forcing the Babylonian empire to surrender. What happened then? Second Chronicles 36:22 tells us: "Now in the first year of Cyrus king of Persia—in order to fulfill the word of the Lord by the mouth of Jeremiah—the Lord stirred up the spirit of Cyrus king of Persia." Was Cyrus a believer? No. On the surface he may have sounded like one, but he was not. He was, however, concerned for the welfare of the Jews. God is not limited to working with His people only. He works in the lives and minds of unbelievers whenever He chooses. He moves the hearts of kings from one plan to another. And this is what He did with Cyrus. Gods ultimate plan was to get the Jews back into their land.

Remember I asked you to take special note of the terms "the house of God" and "the wall"? Here is the reason for that. I wanted you to remember "the house of God" because that is the main subject of the Book of Ezra and "the wall" of Jerusalem because that is the heart of the Book of Nehemiah. The Book of Ezra (which comes just before Nehemiah in the Old Testament), records how the house of God was rebuilt in the city of Jerusalem. But the temple was without protection for ninety years until God led Nehemiah to provide the leadership necessary to build a wall, and it is his account of that project that we call the Book of Nehemiah. — Charles R. Swindoll, *Hand Me Another Brick* (Nashville: Thomas Nelson, 1998).

2. Look at the last verse of chapter 1. What is a cupbearer?

King Artaxerxes is the man to whom Nehemiah reported as cupbearer. Being a cupbearer doesn't sound very impressive. The position sounds comparable to the dishwasher, or at best to the butler or the table waiter. But the cupbearer was far more important than that. The cupbearer tasted the wine before the king drank it, and he tasted the food before the king ate it. If the dinner was poisoned or if somebody was trying to slip the king a "mickey"—no more cupbearer, but long live the king. And through the practice of this custom, an incredible intimacy developed between the taster and the partaker, between the cupbearer and the king. In fact, it has been suggested by ancient historians that the cupbearer, like no one other than the kings wife, was in a position to influence the monarch.

One Old Testament scholar mentions that the cupbearer "was often chosen for his personal beauty and attractions, and in ancient oriental courts was always a person of rank and importance. From the confidential nature of his duties and his frequent access to the royal presence, he possessed great influence." — Charles R. Swindoll, *Hand Me Another Brick* (Nashville: Thomas Nelson, 1998).

3. Nehemiah 1.2. Why did Nehemiah ask this question?

Nehemiah had a cushy job and didn't need to ask. He asked because he cared. God would lead all of us to care about problems outside of our little world.

4. Nehemiah 1.4. What was Nehemiah's first reaction to this bad news?

Prayer was his first reaction, not a last resort. — Josh Hunt (Probably stolen from someone!)

A Serious Leader Goes First to God with the Problem. In verse 5 we hear Nehemiah say, "I beseech Thee, O Lord God of heaven." He prayed. — Charles R. Swindoll, *Hand Me Another Brick* (Nashville: Thomas Nelson, 1998).

5. Verse 5ff. What do we learn about prayer from Nehemiah's prayer?

One of the best ways to improve your prayer life is to study and copy the prayers of the Bible. Our prayers are largely about asking. Biblical prayers nearly always start with praise. They often have a section that goes, "You said, Lord..." The have a God focus: "YOUR servant is praying before YOU for the sake of YOUR name..." (paraphrased with words from other biblical prayers). There is confession—often corporate confession. And, there is a big ask.

6. **The prayer starts the way many biblical prayers start—with worship. The Lord taught us to pray, "Our Father in Heaven, hallowed be Your name..." Why is starting with worship a good idea?**

If you have a big view of God, you will have small problems. If you have a small view of God, you will have big problems.

7. **What is worship? How would you define it?**

Worship is when you're aware that what you've been given is far greater than what you can give. Worship is the awareness that were it not for his touch, you'd still be hobbling and hurting, bitter and broken. Worship is the half-glazed expression on the parched face of a desert pilgrim as he discovers that the oasis is not a mirage.

Worship is the "thank you" that refuses to be silenced. — Max Lucado and Terri A. Gibbs, *Grace for the Moment: Inspirational Thoughts for Each Day of the Year* (Nashville, TN: J. Countryman, 2000), 346.

8. **What are some common misunderstandings of worship?**

I know what a lot of people think worship is, which is singing praises to God, but I feel like worship is a lifestyle. Worship is more than just going to church on Sunday. Worship is letting Jesus Christ control every aspect of your life, and spending time with Him, and doing what you know will please the Lord.

People have a lot of ideas about worship, don't they? Let me tell you what I think worship is. Worship is all that I am responding to all that He is, in gratitude and praise— all that I am responding to all that He, is in gratitude and praise. It is a church service, yes. It is music, yes. It is prayer, yes. But it goes beyond that. All that I am responding to all that He is. And, brothers and sisters, it includes all of life. — Adrian Rogers, "Life's Greatest Privilege," in *Adrian Rogers Sermon Archive* (Signal Hill, CA: Rogers Family Trust, 2017), Jn 4:16–24.

9. How does worship change the worshipper?

There is something about worship.

There is something about looking at God that makes us godlier. There is something about basking in His love that makes us more loving. There is something about thinking about His grace that makes us more gracious. There is something about worship.

On that day we will be like Him, for we will see Him as He is. There is something about seeing Him. There is something about worship. — Josh Hunt, *How to Live the Christian Life,* 2016.

10. What are some practical ways we can make prayer a part of our daily time alone with God?

Got a smart TV or Roku box or something similar (Apple TV or Amazon TV)? Let Chris Tomlin—or your favorite artist lead you in a time of worship. Just do a search on Youtube for Chris Tomlin life.

11. Verse 6. Nehemiah has worshiped, but he isn't ready to ask yet. What comes next?

Notice the words "we" and "I." The confession was not on behalf of someone else's failure. The confession had to do with Nehemiahs part in the problem. What do we do when we are in conflict with another person? We usually blame the other person (our fallen state coming through again). We usually think of six or seven ways the other person has manifested his stubbornness and unwillingness to change, but we seldom consider our part in the problem. But it works both ways. So the very first thing Nehemiah said in regard to the problem was, "Lord, I am culpable. I am not only wanting to be part of the answer, I am confessing myself to be part of the problem."

There may be husband-wife difficulties at your house or strained pupil-teacher relationships at school. There might be strife between a parent and child. And invariably, you will think of your mate or your child or your mom or your teacher or your pupil as being the problem. That is not necessarily the truth.

I plead with you—as you go before God in prayer concerning any unresolved personality conflicts, have the attitude reflected in these words: "Lord, I bring before you these areas where I have caused an irritation. This is my realm of responsibility. I cant change him. But God, I can tell you that this is my part in it; forgive me." — Charles R. Swindoll, *Hand Me Another Brick* (Nashville: Thomas Nelson, 1998).

12. When Jesus taught us to pray, what did he say about confessing our sins and asking for forgiveness?

I once heard of a minister who, short of time and unable to find a parking space, left his car in a No Parking zone. He put a note under the windshield wiper that read, "I have circled the block ten times. I have an appointment to keep. 'Forgive us our debts.' " When he returned, he found a citation from a police officer along with this note: "I've circled this block for ten years. If I don't give you a ticket, I could lose my job. 'Lead us not into temptation.' "

What are our "debts"? The word translated debts could also be translated as sins, trespasses, shortcomings, resentments, what we owe to someone, or a wrong we've done. — Greg Laurie, *New Believer's Guide to Prayer* (Wheaton, IL: Tyndale House Publishers, Inc., 2003), 22.

13. What if I can't think of any sins?

Go through the Ten Commandments. Think about how Jesus reinterpreted them. Go through the Fruit of the Spirit. Have you been 100% loving? Have you been grumpy at all? Have you worried. That is just the first three: love, joy, peace.

14. Verse 8. What do we learn about prayer from this part of Nehemiah's prayer?

Nehemiah didn't stop with confession. Next, he claimed the promise. When he went to God in prayer, he praised the Father, confessed his part in the wrong, and claimed the promise God had given. — Charles R. Swindoll, *Hand Me Another Brick* (Nashville: Thomas Nelson, 1998).

15. What are some of your favorite promises and how could you include them in prayer?

What was the promise? It was twofold. The promise was that if Israel disobeyed, they would go into a foreign land. That had come to pass. The second part was that when that time of captivity was ended, God would bring the Jews back to Jerusalem and protect them. That part was unfulfilled. So Nehemiah was saying, "Lord, the first part is true. We've disobeyed and we've been in captivity. But, Lord, You made a promise to bring us back into the city and protect us, and that has not come to pass yet. I am claiming that it will."

The apostle Paul wrote:

> Yet, with respect to the promise of God, he [Abraham] did not waver in unbelief, but grew strong in faith, giving glory to God, and being fully assured that what He had promised, He was able also to perform. (Rom. 4:20-21)

God does not lightly give out promises. He says, "I promise you that if you will give Me your burden, I will bear it. If you will seek first My kingdom, I will add all these other things to you. If you will make your heart right before Me, I will lead you into a path of stability and prosperity."

That doesn't necessarily mean He will fill your wallet. It does mean He will give you peace—like the world is not able to know. "I will promote you to a place of My level of significance, and you will be satisfied."

Nehemiah said, "Lord, You promised that Your people will be protected in that city, and I'm claiming it right now." — Charles R. Swindoll, *Hand Me Another Brick* (Nashville: Thomas Nelson, 1998).

16. "Grant your servant success today…" Is that a prayer you could confidently pray? Why or why not?

Nehemiah praised God, confessed sins, and spoke with humbleness and respect, but he also asked for big and bold things. He was not afraid to ask that God keep his promises, that God answer his prayers and use him to do great things. May our prayers be as bold. — Doug Bender, *Live Second: 365 Ways to Make Jesus First* (Nashville: Thomas Nelson, 2012).

17. Is there anything off-limits in prayer? Is there anything you shouldn't pray for?

What are you currently facing that needs your prayerful attention? Perhaps it's a career transition; Pray about that. Considering changing churches? Pray about that. Tempted to quit school? Pray about that. Weighing an opportunity to volunteer? Pray about that. Prayerfully ask, "What does the Lord want for my life and what's best for His kingdom?"

"Then you will call on me and come and pray to me, and I will listen to you. You will seek me and find me when you seek me with all your heart" (Jeremiah 29:12-13). — Boyd Bailey, Wisdom for Mothers (Atlanta: Wisdom Hunters, 2011).

18. Do you think we selfishly ask for too much in prayer or timidly ask for too little?

I think our prayers are too timid. We pray for Aunt Susie's ingrown toenail when we need to pray for world revival. We pray to get through this financial hump when we should pray that earth would become a little more like Heaven. God, make us people of big, bold prayers. — Josh Hunt, *The Habit of Discipleship* (Pulpit Press, 2015).

19. **What did you learn about prayer today? How would you like to pray differently?**

20. **How can we pray for each other this week?**

Nehemiah: Building a
Life of Service

Lesson #2: Plan

Nehemiah 2

OPEN

Share your name and... Would you say you are more of a
planner, or do you love spontaneity?

DIG

**1. Context. Refresh our memories. What is the
context? Where are we in the Old Testament story?**

Around 444 BC, a Jewish man named Nehemiah was
charged with the task of rebuilding the wall around
the city of Jerusalem after it had lain in ruins for over
a hundred years. The Jews living in Jerusalem at the
time were content to live with the broken-down wall.
Nehemiah's compelling vision for their future changed
their attitude. In this short but highly effective speech
to the Jews still living in Jerusalem, we find a brilliant
model for casting a compelling vision. As you read, look
for three things: He defined the problem that his vision
addressed. — Andy Stanley, *Making Vision Stick* (Grand
Rapids, MI: Zondervan, 2009).

**2. Overview. What is the story of the book of
Nehemiah?**

Nehemiah's approach was simple and inspiring. He
was first a man of prayer. We see him praying at all
times through the story, understanding that success
would depend on God and not himself. He was also a

man of vision. And above all, Nehemiah was a man of action—he was a doer. He was never overwhelmed by the enormity of the task; instead he was focused on using what he had to accomplish the goal. He divided the bigger goal into smaller pieces. He then developed detailed plans, raised money, and organized people to complete the task. Despite opposition and discouragement, he encouraged and inspired each person to do only what that individual could do—his own part. And he reminded people of the great truths in Scripture. In fact, Nehemiah had the Book of the Law read aloud to the people from daybreak till noon, and we are told that they wept as they listened, repenting of their sins. — Richard Stearns, *The Hole in Our Gospel: What Does God Expect of Us? The Answer That Changed My Life and Might Just Change the World* (Nashville: Thomas Nelson, 2009).

3. Nehemiah, chapter 2. What do we learn about Christian living from this chapter? What is one application?

In the book that bears his name, Nehemiah relates his burden for rebuilding the walls of Jerusalem. The moment he heard of the distress of his city, he began praying, fasting, and seeking God's will (Nehemiah 1:4). His concern deepened until King Artaxerxes noticed it on his face (2:2). Traveling to Jerusalem, Nehemiah surveyed the ruined walls and devised a plan for their rebuilding. At first, he told no one what God had put in his heart to do. But at the right moment he revealed his plan, mobilized the people, and persevered until the work was done.

Have you seen a need? Have you prayed for a burden? Our work for Him isn't a personal ambition we seek. It's a vision He places on our hearts —perhaps to become involved in orphan care, to minister to the homeless, to work with nursery children, to evangelize the lost, to plan a missions trip.

What has God put in your heart to do? What can you do today to make your vision a reality? — David Jeremiah, *Discovering God: 365 Daily Devotions* (Carol Stream, IL: Tyndale, 2015).

4. **What do we learn about success and accomplishing the vision God has for our lives?**

STUDYING NEHEMIAH'S STORY is a little like listening to a concerto. Just as a musical concerto features a soloist, this literary concerto features Nehemiah. He was not the director; God was the Director. The soloist, however, played his instrument with beautiful technique.

A concerto employs a major theme or melody. The main theme of the Book of Nehemiah is leadership. There are counterparts such as planning, prayer, opposition, and government; but in spite of the secondary melodies, the basic theme of leadership comes through over and over again.

Finally, every concerto has at least three major movements, and often each one is played in contrast to the others. One may be quiet and soft; the next, passionate and stirring; and the last may have a touch of all the others, closing with a climactic crescendo.

The same is true in Nehemiah's story of leadership. The first movement takes place from chapter 1 through chapter 2, verse 10, and in it we see Nehemiah playing his part as the king's cupbearer.

Beginning at verse 11 of chapter 2 to the end of chapter 6, there is the soul-stirring second movement of Nehemiah as the builder. The final movement of the book commences when we reach chapter 7 and proceed—in one great crescendo—to the end of the book. In these last five chapters we see Nehemiah as the governor.

If I could press the analogy just a bit further, I'd say that in no other movement does the soloist display greater technique or brilliance than in the second. When Nehemiah became a builder, determined to construct the wall around Jerusalem, I feel he became one of history's great leaders. However, his role as builder didn't begin very eloquently. The first movement ends after having built to a thundering climax in verse 11. You can almost hear the roll of the percussion, the blare of the horns, and the harmony of motion among the strings as Nehemiah proclaims, "I came to Jerusalem."

It is at this point that Nehemiah behaved quite differently from what we might expect. The hurried reader would think that Nehemiah, having reached his destination, would be driven by an inner burning compulsion to pull out the trowel, hire subcontractors, and hang the plumb line; in short, to get someone started on the wall-fast! But, he didn't do that. As a matter of fact, he didn't do anything. The concerto's second movement begins in the latter part of verse 11 with Nehemiah's statement,"... and [I] was there three days." — Charles R. *Swindoll, Hand Me Another Brick* (Nashville: Thomas Nelson, 1998).

5. **In chapter 1 we read and learned from Nehemiah's prayer. Look over that payer. What principles do you recall?**

Nehemiah started with praise. He included identity statement (your servant...). There was repentance, scripture, and a God perspective. Then, there was the big ask.

6. Did Nehemiah pray for miracles?

Our tendency is to pray for miracles. But in most situations, it is more appropriate to pray for opportunities. More than likely you need an opportunity rather than something supernatural. If you are a parent, you probably have a vision for your children. Instead of simply praying that they would become men and women of character, pray for opportunities to build character into their lives. Your vision involves you. You have a role. You have a part to play. If you have a vision for unbelieving friends, don't simply pray that they will be saved. Pray for an opportunity to speak to them about Christ. If you pray for an opportunity, more than likely you will recognize it when God brings it along. — *Visioneering: Your Guide for Discovering and Maintaining Personal Vision*, Andy Stanley

7. What happened after Nehemiah prayed?

What happened after Nehemiah prayed to the Lord? Nothing! At least not right away. Nehemiah's story opened in the month of Chislev (see Neh. 1:1), and it resumes "in the month of Nisan" (Neh. 2:1).

Chislev is December; Nisan is April. For four months nothing happened.

Have you ever had that disillusioning experience? Perhaps you heard the preacher say one Sunday, "Just pray to God; give Him the situation." So you went home and prayed about a frustrating problem and ended with the favorite American prayer: "Lord, give me patience—and I want it NOW!" Then Monday morning came and nothing changed; what's worse, a month from then, nothing had changed. "Lord, are You awake? Did You hear me?" you ask. Another month passes, and then another. That was Nehemiah's experience. — Charles R. Swindoll, *Hand Me Another Brick* (Nashville: Thomas Nelson, 1998).

8. What do we learn about prayer from this story?

The prayer warrior quickly learns the patience of waiting. And so Nehemiah was doing just that—waiting. In the diary he kept, nothing was entered for those four months because nothing happened. He waited. There was no visible glimmer of hope, no change. He kept waiting and trusting and counting on God to move the heart of his superior.

Now look at verse 1 of chapter 2: "And it came about in the month Nisan, in the twentieth year of King Artaxerxes, that wine was before him, and I took up the wine and gave it to the king." The Living Bible emphasizes the waiting period: "One day in April four months later." — Charles R. Swindoll, *Hand Me Another Brick* (Nashville: Thomas Nelson, 1998).

9. Look at verse 7ff. What is the lesson for us here?

"I gave him a definite time."

Do you know that God honors order and organization? Can you imagine what had previously transpired in Nehemiahs mind in order for him to provide an immediate, on-the-spot answer? Nehemiah had a plan. You see, he had been doing more than praying for four months. He had been planning. That in itself was an exercise in faith.He was so sure God would let him go that he even drew up an agenda in case the king asked him how much leave of absence he would need!

Proverbs 16:9 says, "The mind of man plans his way, but the Lord directs his steps."

Going out by faith doesn't mean you're going out in a disorderly or haphazard manner. You think through a project and count the cost financially. (I deal with this issue at length in chapter 7.)

It is of great concern to me that so many people who undertake some project in the Lord's work enter without careful planning. They abruptly begin without thinking through questions such as: "Where will this lead us? How can I express this in clear, unmistakable, concrete terms? What are the costs, the objectives, the possible pitfalls? What process should be used?" I could name a number of individuals or families who entered the ministry with enthusiasm but later dropped out because they had not considered the cost. The most disillusioned people I know are those in the Lord's work who are paying the price of not thinking through their plans.

Admittedly, planning is hard work. Thinking isn't as exciting as involvement, but without it confusion is inevitable. Good leaders do their homework!

Some may read Nehemiah 2:7-9 and think Nehemiah presumptuous. No, he's practical. When King Artaxerxes said, "Fine. You may go," Nehemiah continued, "Now wait a minute, King, before I leave there are a couple of things I want to talk about." — Charles R. Swindoll, *Hand Me Another Brick* (Nashville: Thomas Nelson, 1998).

10. Reading between the lines, it is clear that Nehemiah had developed a plan of action for rebuilding the wall. What did his plan include?

Go ahead and develop a plan. Assuming you had the resources, what would you do? Assuming you had the time, what would you do first? Second? Third? Plan as if you knew someone were going to come along and give you an opportunity to pursue your vision. "Absurd" you say? "A foolish exercise"? Nehemiah didn't think so. He developed a plan. Think about how ludicrous it was for him to even think about having the opportunity and the resources to pursue his vision. Yet, he devised a plan anyway. Nehemiah's Strategy for Rebuilding the Wall in Jerusalem looked something like this:

- Step 1—Convince the king to allow me to leave his service in order to rebuild the wall around a city that in years past posed a military threat to this area.

- Step 2—Convince the king to lend financial support to the building project.

- Step 3—Procure letters from the king to the governors in the surrounding areas asking them to provide me safe conduct along the way.

- Step 4—Work out a deal with Asaph, keeper of the king's forest, to procure enough lumber to build the city gates as well as a home for me.

- Step 5—Ask the king for the title of Governor of Judah.

- Step 6—Organize and equip the inhabitants of Jerusalem.

- Step 7—Begin construction. — *Visioneering: Your Guide for Discovering and Maintaining Personal Vision*, Andy Stanley

11. How do praying and planning work together?

What's he asking for? He's asking for timber to build himself a house. That's a practical mind at work. You see, during these four months of waiting, Nehemiah was planning.

The old Revolutionary War soldiers used to say, "Trust in God, but keep your powder dry." Pray to God, but make your plans, set your sights, think through the hurdles.

Many people in God's work are shortsighted. Imagine Nehemiah's conversation with the first official outside the province of Susa if he had not planned ahead.

"Where are you going?"

"Well, I was hoping by faith to go to Jerusalem."

"Okay, where are your letters?"

"I don't have any letters."

"Then go back and get them."

So, he would have had to go back and start all over.

Nehemiah was unlike the majority of "faith workers." Cant you picture him as he rode out of Susa and approached the first official?

"Here's a letter from the king."

"Who wrote it?"

"Artaxerxes. See . . . right there."

"Oh, man! Go on through."

Next, he entered Asaph's territory. Asaph was probably a negative thinker and maybe a tightwad.

"What do you want?"

"I want some timber."

"Nope! Only by requisition."

"Artaxerxes requisitioned me to have all the timber I want."

I'm sure Asaph checked out that requisition!

That's an example of perfect planning. God honors that kind of thinking. — Charles R. Swindoll, *Hand Me Another Brick* (Nashville: Thomas Nelson, 1998).

12. Can we expect success if we leave out either praying or planning?

Have you made a financial plan for your future? Whether you are young or old, married or single, it is important to establish security for the years ahead.

As we examine today's Scripture passage, we find that there is biblical basis for wise planning. As Jesus spoke poignantly to the crowds around Him, He questioned, "Which of you, intending to build a tower, does not sit down first and count the cost, whether he has enough to finish it?" (Luke 14:28).

Jesus, along with His followers, was familiar with the ridicule persons could receive from failing to complete a project due to poor planning. With this in mind, He encouraged His listeners to include careful calculations in their future plans.

How can you incorporate this advice into your own life? First, realize that God expects us to not only trust Him but also actively make plans under His counsel. Second, we should study the Scriptures to develop a Christ-centered strategy of financial protection. Finally, we must subject our financial matters to the lordship of Jesus Christ.

Praying over decisions that will affect your future, and possibly the future of your children, is essential. "Be anxious for nothing, but in everything by prayer and supplication, with thanksgiving, let your requests be made known to God" (Philippians 4:6).

As you plan with God's will in mind, He will honor your diligence and obedience. — Charles F. Stanley, *Pathways to His Presence* (Nashville, TN: Thomas Nelson Publishers, 2006), 136.

13. What consequences come to the person who prays but fails to plan?

The first thing I want you to notice is that he is systematic. This word wiles is the word we get our word method from. It's even the word that the Methodists get the name of their church from. The Methodists are Methodists because they are methodical in doing their work. That's where the name came: They had good methods, and they called themselves Methodists. And every Baptist church ought to be a "methodist" church. Every Baptist church ought to have methods and use methods; we ought to have plans. Somebody said, "To fail to plan is to plan to fail"—and I believe that is true. But whether or not we are methodical, I can tell you that the devil is methodical. This word methodeia is the word that we get our word methodical from: "the wiles of the devil." — Adrian Rogers, "The Christian's Warfare," in *Adrian Rogers Sermon Archive* (Signal Hill, CA: Rogers Family Trust, 2017), Eph 6:10–22.

14. What happens to the person who plans, but fails to pray?

Sometimes we do not get the desires of our hearts for reasons known only to God. However, I believe that many times we do not get our desires simply because we fail to pray effectively.

The Bible is filled with images of God's people coming before Him in humble entreaty. A desperate ruler, a drowning prophet, and a barren woman all petitioned the King, and the King responded. We are exhorted to "present [our] requests to God" (Phil. 4:6). We are promised that if we ask "it will be given" (Mt. 7:7). We are reminded that the "prayer of a righteous man is powerful and effective" (Jas. 5:16). But unfortunately, our everyday experience of petitionary prayer may lack power and rarely seem effective. — Discipleship Journal, *Issue 97* (January/February 1997) (NavPress, 1997).

15. Which are you more likely to neglect—praying or planning?

Planning is a prerequisite for anyone who desires to get results. But, prayerful planning is essential to experience God's best. After all, His best is the goal for the follower of Jesus Christ. Otherwise, we are limited to what only our efforts can produce. This self-imposed limitation is misery compared to partnering with the Almighty. We can work hard to plan—and sincerely produce a best-laid plan—but make the mistake of asking God to bless the plan after the fact. This presumes on God. He is not thrilled with the presumption of His blessing. Presumption communicates distrust and disrespect. He may choose to bless the unprayed plan, but why take the chance? And why take the credit? He will share His glory with no one.

So, a prayerless plan will leave you in a perilous position. — Boyd Bailey, *Infusion* (Atlanta: Wisdom Hunters, 2011).

16. Proverbs 15.22 is a good cross-reference. What do we learn about wise planning from this verse?

Wise planning is collaborative in nature as it understands the wisdom found in diverse perspectives. It is not intimidated by input but invites it. Otherwise, we are limited by our own ideas, experience, and intellect. Wise planning is a way to assure success and minimize risk. We are presumptuous and irresponsible not to pay the price of planning. Even King David validated the plan with the people:

"The plan seemed right both to the king and to the whole assembly" (2 Chronicles 30:4). — Boyd Bailey, *Seeking God in the Proverbs* (Atlanta: Wisdom Hunters, 2013).

17. Verses 17. How was Nehemiah able to persuade people to do what had been undone for years?

To cast a convincing vision, you have to define the problem that your vision addresses. For Nehemiah the problem was obvious. Jerusalem was in ruins! That was a problem for the Jewish people. But it wasn't until he drew their attention to it and put forth a plan of action that they felt compelled to do something about it.

Every vision is a solution to a problem. If your vision doesn't get traction, something that needs to happen won't happen. A problem will continue to go unaddressed.To make your vision stick, your audience needs to understand what's at stake. It's the what's at stake issue that grabs people's hearts. Only a clear explanation of the problem will cause people to sit up and say, "Something must be done!" If your target audience doesn't know what's at stake, the vision will never stick.

So what problem does your vision propose to solve? Every successful organization—for profit or nonprofit— is viewed by its customers or clients as a solution to a problem. If you don't believe me, Google "business solutions. " You'll get more than 440,000 results.Why? Because a business knows its future hinges on the perception that its product is a solution to someone's problem. The same is true of your vision. Buy-in by others hinges on your ability to convince them that you are offering a solution to a problem they are convinced needs to be solved.

To cast your vision in a convincing manner, you need to be able to answer these two questions: What is the need or problem my vision addresses? and What will happen if those needs or problems continue to go unaddressed? — Andy Stanley, Making Vision Stick (Grand Rapids, MI: Zondervan, 2009).

18. Note the phrase, "we will no longer be in disgrace." What does that mean?

The third component to a convincing vision is the reason something must be done now. You have to present people with a reason for your vision. You have to answer the questions: Why must we do this? Why must we do this now?

Nehemiah's reason was wrapped up in this theologically pregnant phrase, "and we will no longer be in disgrace." Space does not allow me to fully explain the significance of those eight words. The bottom line: the Jews knew that the city of Jerusalem was meant to reflect the greatness of their God. As long as the city was in disarray, it reflected poorly on God. Something had to be done. — Andy Stanley, *Making Vision Stick* (Grand Rapids, MI: Zondervan, 2009).

19. What do you want to recall from today's study?

20. How can we pray for each other today?

Nehemiah: Building a Life of Service

Lesson #3: Persist

Nehemiah 4.1 – 9; 14 - 18

OPEN

Share your name and one thing that fires you up, or, one thing that tends to discourage you.

DIG

1. Nehemiah 4.1 – 9. What do we learn about how the godly are successful from this passage?

THE DRAMA OF NEHEMIAH 4 ABOUNDS with lessons and illustrations of various truths. But we must not forget that what to us is a dramatic narrative was to those experiencing it days of brutally hard work, high tension, genuine fear, insecurity, rising faith, dirt and grime. Nevertheless, some lessons transcend the ages:

(1) Among the hardest things to endure is derisory contempt. That is what Nehemiah and the Jews faced from Sanballat, Tobiah, and the rest (4:1–3). The Judeo-Christian heritage of Western nations was until recent decades so strong that many Christians were shielded from such scorn. No more. We had better get used to what our brothers and sisters in Christ in other lands and centuries handle better than we. — D. A. Carson, *For the Love of God: A Daily Companion for Discovering the Riches of God's Word., vol. 2* (Wheaton, IL: Crossway Books, 1998), 25.

2. **Read for application. What application can you find
    in this passage?**

As Nehemiah led the others in building the wall, he had
his eyes on the baton of the Director.

Do you realize you can have your eyes in various
directions in the Christian life? You can have your eyes
glued on some other person. If you do, before long you
will be disappointed or even disillusioned because that
person will fail. Never set your eyes on some church staff
member or church officer or another friend. That's the
best way I know of crippling your walk. Instead, steady
your focus on God.

You can have your eyes on your own situation and
become absorbed in self-pity, or you can get your eyes
on yourself and be puffed with pride or demoralized by
insecurity. With your eyes on yourself, you are constantly
comparing your life with someone else's. You will never
stay balanced while fighting the comparison battle.

The choice is yours. You can permit your eyes to wander
aimlessly, or you can simply look up and fix your eyes
on the Director. Though you might have what you call
an insignificant part in the total orchestration, you will
never miss your cue. — Charles R. Swindoll, *Hand Me
Another Brick* (Nashville: Thomas Nelson, 1998).

3. **Who was Sanballat? What do we know about
    Sanballat?**

Notice that right away opposition comes! It never
fails. There is direct criticism of the plan. As soon as
the rebuilding crews rolled up their sleeves, they were
opposed. Murphy's Law could again be heard: "But
when Sanballat the Horonite, and Tobiah the Ammonite

official, and Geshem the Arab heard it, they mocked us and despised us" (v. 19). — Charles R. Swindoll, Hand Me Another Brick (Nashville: Thomas Nelson, 1998).

4. What is it that makes criticism so much fun? Why it so popular to be critical?

The Hebrew term for mock means "to stammer, to stutter, to utter repeatedly words of derision." Sanballat and Tobiah held their heads high, looked down their noses, and scoffed at that little group of Jews, saying, "You're out of your minds. You'll never be able to do it. After all, you're rebelling against the king, aren't you?" — Charles R. Swindoll, *Hand Me Another Brick* (Nashville: Thomas Nelson, 1998).

5. Does anyone remember that famous quote by Roosevelt... "It is not the critic that counts..."

It is not the critic who counts; not the man who points out how the strong man stumbles, or where the doer of deeds could have done them better. The credit belongs to the man who is actually in the arena, whose face is marred by dust and sweat and blood; who strives valiantly; who errs, who comes short again and again, because there is no effort without error and shortcoming; but who does actually strive to do the deeds; who knows great enthusiasms, the great devotions; who spends himself in a worthy cause; who at the best knows in the end the triumph of high achievement, and who at the worst, if he fails, at least fails while daring greatly, so that his place shall never be with those cold and timid souls who neither know victory nor defeat.

https://www.goodreads.com/quotes/7-it-is-not-the-critic-who-counts-not-the-man

6. How do you deal with critics? How should we deal with critics?

Those of us who have known Billy Graham for many years have admired the way he has not answered his critics. Sometimes if a racehorse pays too much attention to a horsefly, it makes the fly too important. Some people's only taste of success is the bite they take out of someone whom they perceive is doing more than they are.

It's helpful to have a friend or two who can help you sort the minor criticisms from the major ones. Then you can treat minor criticisms in a minor way—such as ignore them. But you can also take seriously major criticisms that will grow and can't be ignored. Honest people with a fresh perspective can help you recognize what is a deep and powerful current and what is just a surface wave.

One way I limit the criticism I accept is to refuse any that distracts from the organization's main purpose.

Bill Waugh, owner of a restaurant chain, was asked to become chairman of The Salvation Army. He chose as his theme "Keep the main thing the main thing." By that he meant, "Keep the purpose of the organization clearly in mind and do not get diverted from it." — Fred Smith, "The Care and Feeding of Critics," in *Leading Your Church through Conflict and Reconciliation: 30 Strategies to Transform Your Ministry, ed.* Marshall Shelley, *vol. 1,*

Library of Leadership Development (Minneapolis, MN: Bethany House Publishers, 1997), 267–268.

7. **Verse 6. What happens at the half-way point of any project?**

We get tired. We have been at it so long that the initial burst of enthusiasm is gone. But, we are not close enough to the end to be energized by the light at the end of the tunnel. It is a real good time to get discouraged.

8. **Half way through a diet is a good time to quit. Half way through school is a good time to get discouraged. Half way through a marriage is a good time to have an affair. Half way... the most dangerous of times. Why is this?**

It was before the wall was half finished that the workers began to be bombarded with the sarcastic words of the critics: "Now it came about that when Sanballat heard that we were rebuilding the wall, he became furious" (4:1). What prompted the opposition was the progress in the construction project. One would think that seeing this small band of people succeeding in a massive project would evoke admiration. But this was not so. You see, the heart of the habitual critic resists change. To him, change is a threat.In any organization, those who are most critical of change are those who are most inflexible. They resist change, and they become especially suspicious of changes that lead to progress and growth. — Charles R. Swindoll, *Hand Me Another Brick* (Nashville: Thomas Nelson, 1998).

9. Verse 9. We pray to our God AND posted a guard. What is the abiding principle from this verse?

Notice that little word, "and." As in, "both/and." Nehemiah both prayed to his God and posted a guard. He was spiritual enough to pray. He was practical enough to post a guard. He was not so heavenly minded he was no Earthly good. He was a deeply spiritual man with a cool head on his shoulders.

Why is it that some would ask us to choose between the two? Why is it that some would say that it has to be either/or? Why can't we be both deeply spiritual people with clear headed thinking as well? Is God the God of muddled thinking? Who created our minds? Who created our world that rewards practical action, assessment and feedback?

I believe God would have us be both: deeply spiritual and profoundly practical. Pray to our God and post a guard. — Josh Hunt, *Enjoying God* (Josh Hunt, 2000).

10. What bad things happen if we pray to our God but do not post a guard?

There is an old story about a man who carried the doctrine of God's sovereignty to such an extreme that he drifted into a sort of divine fatalism. One day, walking down a flight of stairs, he carelessly stumbled and fell headlong to the bottom of the staircase. Picking himself up, he gingerly felt his bruises and said to himself, "Well, I'm glad that one is over."

If we are not careful, you and I can, like the foolish man in the story, drift into a fatalistic attitude about the sovereignty of God. A student who fails an important exam tries to excuse himself by saying, "Well, God is sovereign, and He determined that I should fail that exam." A driver can cause an auto accident and, in his own mind, evade his carelessness by attributing the accident to the sovereignty of God. Obviously both attitudes are unbiblical and foolish, yet we can easily drift into them. — Jerry Bridges, *Is God Really in Control?: Trusting God in a World of Hurt* (Colorado Springs, CO: NavPress, 2006), 67–68.

11. What bad things happen if we post a guard but fail to pray?

Note Nehemiah's response to the threatened attack. His people prayed and posted a guard. He recognized his dependence on God, but he also accepted his responsibility to work—to stand guard.

Today, we would tend to divide into two camps. The more "spiritual" people would call an all-night prayer meeting. To them, posting a guard would be depending on human effort instead of God. The "practical" ones among us would do a fine job organizing the guard and assigning everyone to various watches, but they would be too busy to pray.

Nehemiah and his people did both. They recognized their dependence on God, but they also understood they were depending on Him to enable and help them, not to do their work for them. — Jerry Bridges, *Holiness Day by Day: Transformational Thoughts for Your Spiritual Journey,* ed. Thomas Womack (Colorado Springs, CO: NavPress, 2008), 84.

12. Does God normally send protection to a people who *don't* post a guard?

There are instances in the Old Testament where God miraculously intervened and actually fought the battle for Israel (such as 2 Chronicles 20). But these are the exception, not the rule. However—and this is an important statement—there is not a single instance in New Testament teaching on holiness where we are taught to depend on the Holy Spirit without a corresponding exercise of discipline on our part. — Jerry Bridges, *Holiness Day by Day: Transformational Thoughts for Your Spiritual Journey,* ed. Thomas Womack (Colorado Springs, CO: NavPress, 2008), 84.

13. What is the emotion of verse 10?

See the word failing? The original text says "stumbling, tottering, staggering." "These people, Nehemiah, have been working a long time, and they are getting tired." How long had they been building this wall? Verse 6 tells us they were halfway through: "The whole wall was joined together to half its height." The newness had worn off.

Let me make it even more practical. Have you ever bought a new car? Can you remember when it lost its newness? Probably when you got halfway through paying for it.

Let's say you have undertaken a difficult project of redecorating your home. When is the most discouraging time? Usually it's when you are halfway through, and the mess gets to be more than you can handle.

Maybe you've tried mountain climbing. You look up and say, "Oh, maybe an hour—an hour and thirty minutes at the most." Five hours later, when you're halfway up, you look back down and say, "I think the Lord is leading us back!"

Halfway is discouraging!

"Were getting tired, Nehemiah. The strength of these who have been working is failing." A loss of strength takes an emotional toll on our bodies. — Charles R. Swindoll, *Hand Me Another Brick* (Nashville: Thomas Nelson, 1998).

14. Look back at verse 6. What is the contrasting mood in these two verses? What happened?

Perhaps the most devastating cause of discouragement is an obvious loss of confidence. Nehemiahs workers became weary and disillusioned. The wall was halfway up. Rubbish was strewn everywhere. They voiced their feelings by sadly observing, "We ourselves are unable to rebuild the wall" (v. 10). When you lose strength and you lose vision, then you lose confidence. And when you've lost confidence, discouragement is winking at you around the corner.

These Jews had built the wall to half its height because the people "had a mind to work." The Hebrew reads,"... the people had a heart to work." But now they lost their heart When you lose your confidence, you lose your heart; you lose your motivation. A number of things can cause that, but there is always an empty feeling—that overwhelming, discouraging sense that you are never going to catch up. — Charles R. Swindoll, *Hand Me Another Brick* (Nashville: Thomas Nelson, 1998).

15. "So much rubble." Repeat that phrase three times. What is the lesson for us?

Did you notice what Judah said? "Yet there is much rubbish" (4:10). The word yet is significant because it connects the thought with the previous statement. The burden bearers' strength was expended and began to fail; yet, in spite of all the work, there's a lot of rubbish. The Hebrew word for rubbish means "dry earth, debris."

"We look around, Nehemiah, and all we can see is debris—dirt, broken stones, hard, dried chunks of mortar. It's getting tiring.

There's too much rubbish."

Rubbish and discouragement are Siamese twins.

The builders had lost the vision of the completed wall. A perfect illustration of this myopic outlook is the young mother who has changed what seems to be fifty or sixty diapers in one day. She looks at the situation and says, "There's too much rubbish, too much mess, too many diapers, too much work." What has she lost? She has lost the vision of that growing child and the delight of introducing her son or daughter to society. She has lost her whole sense of fulfillment in the motherhood role because of the current "rubbish."

Some of you are involved in jobs right now that are very demanding—-even threatening—and there are difficult people to work with. Or maybe the tasks seem endless. You can easily begin to lose the whole vision of your work because of the "rubbish" surrounding you. — Charles R. Swindoll, *Hand Me Another Brick* (Nashville: Thomas Nelson, 1998).

16. Does discouragement visit God-followers?

You might think that discouragement is only for those not walking with God. That's not true. Some Christian leaders admit that occasionally times of discouragement have been signals from God announcing a whole new direction and plan. Strange though it may seem, discouragement, brought on by a removal of our tangible securities, has been known to usher in incredible achievements.

Such was the admission of Charles Haddon Spurgeon, one of the greatest spokesmen for Christ that English-speaking people ever heard. Here is his own admission:

> Before any great achievement, some measure of depression is very usual. . . . Such was my experience when I first became a pastor in London. My success appalled me, and the thought of the career which seemed to open up, so far from elating me, cast me into the lowest depth, out of which I uttered my miserere and found no room for a gloria in excelsis. Who was I that I should continue to lead so great a multitude? I would betake me to my village obscurity, or emigrate to America and find a solitary nest in the backwoods where I might be sufficient for the things that were demanded of me. It was just then the curtain was rising on my lifework. . . . This depression comes over me whenever the Lord is preparing a larger blessing for my ministry.

Have you ever wanted to run away? What a desire we have to escape, to get away from life's demands. But after enduring the discouragement we could be led to an opportunity offering unbelievable fulfillment. — Charles R. Swindoll, *Hand Me Another Brick* (Nashville: Thomas Nelson, 1998).

17. What are some causes of discouragement?

Well, number one, there's a physical cure: Renew your strength. Now, look, if you will, in verses 21 and 22: "So we laboured in the work:"—now you have to keep on working—"and half of them held the spears from the rising of the morning till the stars appeared. Likewise at the same time I said unto the people, Let every one with his servant lodge within Jerusalem, that in the night they may be a guard to us, and labour on the day." (Nehemiah 4:21–22) That is, "Go lie down and get some rest."

If you're discouraged, your problem may be as simple as this: that you just need to rest. You need to change your diet. You need to get some exercise. You maybe just need to go to the doctor and get a checkup. It may be physical. It may be emotional. Maybe you need a checkup from the neck up. But go and get a checkup physically. When you get worn out physically and the problem of fatigue comes, you can get discouraged. — Adrian Rogers, "How to Get up When You Are Down," in *Adrian Rogers Sermon Archive* (Signal Hill, CA: Rogers Family Trust, 2017), Ne 4:6–22.

18. What is the cure to discouragement?

There's an interesting story in the Old Testament about another man, a prophet whose name was Elijah. Elijah was a man of God, but he got so discouraged one time he wanted to die. And put in your margin 1 Kings 19, and let me read that to you. First Kings chapter 19, beginning in verse 4—it speaks of Elijah, and it says, "But he himself went a day's journey into the wilderness, and came and sat down under a juniper tree: and he requested for himself that he might die; and said It is enough; now, O LORD, take away my life; for I am not better than my fathers." Evidently, he thought he was somewhat better than his ancestors, and he found out he was just the same—that he was a human being. And now, notice in verse 5: "And as he lay an slept under a juniper tree, behold, then an angel touched him, and said unto him, Arise and eat. And he looked, and, behold, there was a cake baken on the coals, and a cruse of water at his head. And he did eat and drink, and laid him down again. And the angel of the LORD came again the second time, and touched him, and said, Arise and eat; because the journey is too great for thee. And he arose, and did eat and drink, and went in the strength of that meat forty days and forty nights unto Horeb the mount of God." (1 Kings 19:4–8)

Now Elijah had a pity party. He got so discouraged that he said he wanted to die. Of course, he really didn't mean that. He'd just run cross-country to get away from Jezebel. If he had wanted to die, all he would have had to do was stand still, and Jezebel would have taken care of him. She'd already said, "I'm going to make you a foot shorter at the top; I'm going to take off your head." But he's just drinking from the intoxicating cup of self-pity. But he's worn out. I mean, he's been without food; he's been without rest; he's been without sleep. And he gets under the juniper tree and he says, "Oh, I wish I could die!" And he even prays to die.

Now we thank God for answered prayer. Have you ever thanked God for unanswered prayer? Did you know we'd be in the soup if God answered all our prayers? Thank God He doesn't! He said, "God, I want to die." God said, "You're not going to die; you're going to sleep. Lie down, son, and sleep." And then He said, "Wake up and eat." And then He says, "Lie down and sleep." And then He says, "Wake up and eat."

You know, probably, you just might need a vacation. You might just need to take some time off and let some things go. And, you know, Elijah thought he was the only prophet of the Lord. The Lord said, "You know, I've got a lot around here besides you, Elijah. I've got 450 people who haven't bowed their knee to Baal. Go to sleep and get some rest." The Bible says, "It is vain for you to rise up early, to sit up late, to eat the bread of sorrows: for so he giveth his beloved sleep." (Psalm 127:2) And maybe that's what you need; maybe you just simply need some rest.

Let me give you some advice: Never make a major decision when you're fatigued—just don't do it; when you're depressed—just don't do it. And, you know, what we need to do, all of us in this church—Brother Bob, you and I have been talking about it—we're going to try to get our people in this church healthy—physically and financially. I mean, you know—God's people, you know—what the big sin would be? Baptists, you know, we don't drink; we don't gamble. So what do we do? We gorge. — Adrian Rogers, "How to Get up When You Are Down," in Adrian *Rogers Sermon Archive* (Signal Hill, CA: Rogers Family Trust, 2017), Ne 4:6–22.

19. What do you want to remember from today's conversation?

20. How can we encourage one another in prayer this week?

Nehemiah: Building a Life of Service

Lesson #4: Protect

Nehemiah 5

OPEN

Share your name and one thing that is on your mind these days.

DIG

1. **Review / context. Look back over the first four chapters of Nehemiah. What is the story up until now?**

    The distribution of material in Nehemiah 1–6 is interesting. One chapter is given to Nehemiah's reaction to the challenge to build Jerusalem's walls; one chapter to his audience with Artaxerxes, his trip to Jerusalem, and his nighttime inspection of the ruins; a third chapter to the way the walls were built. But then three whole chapters (chaps. 4–6) discuss the opposition Nehemiah encountered while building the wall and how he dealt with it. — James Montgomery Boice, *Nehemiah: An Expositional Commentary* (Grand Rapids, MI: BakerBooks, 2005), 59.

2. **Building the wall has not gone without push back. How is the push back in this chapter different from what has come before?**

    Suddenly, to judge from the tone of chapter 5, a new form of opposition erupted and from an unexpected source. The first two forms of opposition had been from without, from Israel's enemies. This new form was from within. It arose because of wrong conduct by some of the Jewish people themselves.

Isn't that the way it always is? You are engaged in some important work. You have been opposed by people who are not Christians and do not share the vision. You have overcome that form of opposition and are pressing on, when suddenly there is a problem within the church or Christian community itself. Often this threat is more of a problem than the external threat. It had been true of Israel before this. During the days of the monarchy, the Jewish states had been opposed by their pagan neighbors. There had been many wars. But when God sent prophets to recall the people to righteousness, it was not the pagans who killed God's messengers but the Jews themselves. In the same way, an examination of church history will show that the most successful attacks upon the church have come not from unbelievers but from those within, from people who have professed to know God and Jesus Christ. They have been from "Christians" promoting heresy or "believers" denouncing, persecuting, or even killing other Christians.
— James Montgomery Boice, *Nehemiah: An Expositional Commentary* (Grand Rapids, MI: BakerBooks, 2005), 59–60.

3. How does this relate to us? What is the greatest hinderance of the church today?

Who is responsible for most opposition to Christian work today? Is it the government with its radical "separation of church and state" policies? Is it the American Civil Liberties Union with its strong bias against religion? These can be sources of genuine opposition, and they are. But is it not true that the greatest opposition to

Christian work today is from those within the church who want a form of godliness but who reject genuine Christianity?

The cartoon character Pogo said, "We have met the enemy and he is us." Nehemiah found this to be the case in his day, and we will too. — James Montgomery Boice, *Nehemiah: An Expositional Commentary* (Grand Rapids, MI: BakerBooks, 2005), 60.

4. Nehemiah 5.1. Read for emotion. What is the tone?

The suddenness and extent of this accusation seem to have taken everyone by surprise. Without warning, something akin to internal warfare is taking place as family groups from the poorer communities openly accuse the landowners and merchant classes of greed and exploitation. The two verses that open up chapter 5 are merely a summary of serious discontent: families who are railing at each other and looking to Nehemiah for an immediate solution. — Derek W. H. Thomas, *Ezra & Nehemiah*, ed. Richard D. Phillips, Philip Graham Ryken, and Iain M. Duguid, *Reformed Expository Commentary* (Phillipsburg, NJ: P&R Publishing, 2016), 271.

5. Is this a story about rich people or poor people?

These verses describe a classic example of the gap between rich and poor and the way the rich sometimes tend to control things so that they get richer while the poor get poorer. It was a case of pure exploitation, and what made it worse was that it occurred within the Jewish community among those who should have been helping one another.

Originally the Jews who had returned to Israel from Babylon were well-off. Cyril Barber reminds us that, according to the first chapters of Ezra, those who had come back from the exile returned with many worldly goods. Ezra gave an inventory of their possessions, reporting in summary that there were fifty-four hundred articles of gold and silver (Ezra 1:11). In addition, King Cyrus had himself opened his treasury and had contributed "the articles belonging to the temple of the LORD, which Nebuchadnezzar had carried away from Jerusalem" (Ezra 1:7; cf. 2 Chron. 36:18; Dan. 1:1–2). Once in Jerusalem, many of the Jews were either wealthy enough or had prospered sufficiently to panel their homes, a luxury at one time reserved only for kings (Hag. 1:4). When the temple was built, the people gave generously for its embellishment (Neh. 7:71–72).

Besides, only thirteen years before Nehemiah's arrival, a second group of exiles had returned with Ezra, and these had brought additional "silver and gold" and "the freewill offerings of the people" left in Babylon (Ezra 7:16). Other gifts from Babylon seem to have been arriving regularly (Zech. 6:10). — James Montgomery Boice, *Nehemiah: An Expositional Commentary* (Grand Rapids, MI: BakerBooks, 2005), 60–61.

6. What complaints do the people have for Nehemiah? Let's make a list.

There were several factors. One of the cries of the people recorded in chapter 5 mentions famine. A lack of rain and the consequent failure of the crops was one problem. Others complained about the king's taxation, though scholars generally agree that this was not particularly burdensome, at least not for any but the extremely poor. These were contributing factors, but the real problem—which Nehemiah seemed to get to immediately—is that the wealthier Jews had been exploiting those who were less well-off and actually reducing some of them to the desperate state of slavery. Exploiting? Perhaps that is too strong a word. The wealthy would never have used it. They would have claimed that they were merely lending money in perfectly legal ways, perhaps even doing it to "help" their poorer countrymen. But whether it was technically legal or not, the rich were certainly taking advantage of the situation. As Nehemiah says later, their actions were "not right" (v. 9). — James Montgomery Boice, *Nehemiah: An Expositional Commentary* (Grand Rapids, MI: BakerBooks, 2005), 61.

7. Compare group #1 with group #2. Who has the bigger problem?

A famine is taking place, necessitating the mortgaging of their property as security against loans to buy grain for planting. This may have been a condition that had existed before Nehemiah arrived in the city, and these families may have been in debt before the wall project was suggested. Their condition is not as serious as that of the first group—who had no money at all—but worries are now mounting among them regarding the means to pay off their mortgages from the harvest, which was a few months away. Poor as these crops must have been in these conditions, the prospect for a decent harvest sufficient to repay the Jews' loans was now a forlorn expectation. The consequences of unpaid debts would be dire: families would be expected to sell their children as temporary servants in order to pay the debt. But if conditions prevailed and their land became forfeit, they were facing irreversible debt-servitude. — Derek W. H. Thomas, *Ezra & Nehemiah*, ed. Richard D. Phillips, Philip Graham Ryken, and Iain M. Duguid,

Reformed Expository Commentary (Phillipsburg, NJ: P&R Publishing, 2016), 271.

8. Look at groups #2 and #3. What hope did they have of paying off this debt?

Israel provided legal code for these circumstances, legislating a fair period of labor service to the creditor as well as a time limit on the servitude for the debt slave. No one could serve more than six years. When a person was freed, he went out debt-free (Ex. 21:2–11; 22:25–27; Deut. 15:1–18; 24:10–13). The poor had rights, therefore, enshrined in the law. In addition, Leviticus 25 gave further stipulations concerning the possibility of forfeiture of land and property because of economic circumstances. If a person fell into poverty and lost his field or other property, there had to be opportunities to return that land to the original owner. It could be bought back at a reasonable price simply by the original owner's encountering better economic times than the person to whom he had sold it. It could be bought by a kinsman-redeemer, someone who came and bought the land so that the property did not have to be sold to someone outside the family. Or at the fifty-year Jubilee, at the seventh of the seven Sabbath years, the land would automatically revert, according to the law of Moses, back to the family of those who had originally owned it. Evidently, even if these Jews adhered to the Jubilee-year law (which is doubtful), it was probably too far away to alleviate their immediate concerns. — Derek W. H. Thomas, Ezra & Nehemiah, ed. Richard D. Phillips, Philip Graham Ryken, and Iain M. Duguid, Reformed Expository Commentary (Phillipsburg, NJ: P&R Publishing, 2016), 271–272.

9. Verse 6 describes Nehemiah as very angry. Was this a good thing? Was this the right response to the situation?

As I have read the various commentaries on Nehemiah, I have been amused to see how much contemporary writers struggle over Nehemiah's anger. This is because anger seems basically wrong to them. John White wrestles with whether Nehemiah's anger was just or merely carnal, and with whether, assuming it was at least largely carnal, it was better to express or repress it.

Cyril Barber recognizes the difference between righteous and unrighteous anger and finds Nehemiah's response to be that of a godly man. But he regards anger as so much of a problem that he interrupts his exposition with a section on "how to handle it." In fact, it is not only commentators who have struggled with Nehemiah's anger. Translators have done it too. For example, at verse 7 the New English Bible reads, "I mastered my feelings and reasoned with the nobles," implying that the anger of verse 6 was wrong. The New International Version is surely closer to the truth when it says, "I pondered them [the charges] in my mind and then accused the nobles." The Revised Standard Version states forcefully, "I took counsel with myself, and I brought charges." — James Montgomery Boice, *Nehemiah: An Expositional Commentary* (Grand Rapids, MI: BakerBooks, 2005), 62.

10. When is anger a good thing? When is it a bad thing?

There is a great difference between righteous and unrighteous anger, and we are frequently angry only in the second sense, when something is offensive to us personally. But while we need to be warned against such anger, we also need urging to be angry when righteous anger is appropriate.

Some years ago Franky Schaeffer, son of the late evangelical author and Christian apologist Francis A. Schaeffer, wrote a book entitled A Time for Anger: The Myth of Neutrality. It began, "There are times in which anyone with a shred of moral principle should be profoundly angry. We live in such times." — James Montgomery Boice, *Nehemiah: An Expositional Commentary* (Grand Rapids, MI: BakerBooks, 2005), 62.

11. What is not-good about the Christian who never gets angry?

The first recorded response of Nehemiah is one of anger (Neh. 5:6). The exploitation of the poor angers him, and he shows it. This is not a time for maudlin sentiment. It is a sickly Christianity that insists that the initial reaction to every circumstance be acquiescent forgiveness! It was not the reaction of Paul when confronting the hypocrisy and gospel-threatening behavior of Peter in Antioch, where he refused to eat with the Gentiles when Jewish-Christian leaders from the church in Jerusalem arrived for what looked like an inspection (Gal. 2:7–14). Nor, more importantly, was it Jesus' reaction when encountering money-changers at the entrance to the temple, overturning their money-laden tables and castigating them for turning the temple into a den of thieves (Mark 11:15–17). Or his reaction to the indifference of the Jews in the synagogue to a man with a withered hand, preferring to argue about the propriety of healing on the Sabbath than to see him relieved of his suffering. The text reads that Jesus looked at them "with anger" (Mark 3:5). We are to be angry without sinning, Paul exhorts (Eph. 4:26). And Nehemiah's reaction is the right response to immoral conduct that hurts others.
— Derek W. H. Thomas, *Ezra & Nehemiah*, ed. Richard D. Phillips, Philip Graham Ryken, and Iain M. Duguid,

Reformed Expository Commentary (Phillipsburg, NJ: P&R Publishing, 2016), 274–275.

12. What did Nehemiah do when he got angry? What is the lesson for us?

Now look at the next verse. I love this: "And I consulted with myself" (v. 7). Aren't you glad that's in there? Yes, he got mad, but he thought before he spoke. In those moments of self-consultation, God was able to speak to Nehemiah about what to say next. Self-control is a virtue the leader cannot afford to be without.

Nehemiah, when very angry, found a way to cool down. He consulted with himself and listened to God's voice. The Hebrew word for consult, as used here, means "to give one self-advice, to counsel oneself." That's the very best thing to do when you get mad. You need to have a quiet place where you can lay all the emotions of your soul before God. Nobody hears but God. Marvelous therapy comes from sharing with God the hurt and the anger as you "consult with yourself" before you face the situation head-on. — Charles R. Swindoll, *Hand Me Another Brick* (Nashville: Thomas Nelson, 1998).

13. What does the Bible teach about charging interest?

Why does God give those explicit instructions to potential creditors? Verse 20 continues: "So that the Lord your God may bless you in all that you undertake." God was saying that He wanted His people, the Jews, to be unique. In effect, He was saying, "I will bless you, and you wont have to charge interest to your own brothers. You will maintain a distinction that will cause the foreigner to rub his bearded chin and say, 'How in the world can that nation continue?' And you can answer, 'The Lord, our God provides our needs without interest among ourselves.' That will make you distinct. Then the Lord your God will bless you in all that you undertake."

In between Exodus and Deuteronomy is a passage in Leviticus 25 that may also have been in Nehemiah's mind.

> Now in case a countryman of yours [a fellow Jew] becomes poor and his means with regard to you falter, then you are to sustain him like a stranger or a sojourner, that he may live with you. Do not take usurious interest from him, but revere your God, that your countryman may live with you. You shall not give him your silver at interest, nor your food for gain. [Don't give him one bushel of grain, expecting one and a halfback. Give him one for one.] I am the Lord your God, who brought you out of the land of Egypt to give you the land of Canaan and to be your God. And if a countryman of yours becomes so poor with regard to you that he sells himself to you, you shall not subject him to a slave's service. He shall be with you as a hired man, as if he were a sojourner with you. (vv. 35-40)

No Jew was ever to enslave another Jew. Such action was evidence of an absence of love and concern for his brother. Their family love was to supersede love of money. God's instructions (which they willfully disobeyed) would have protected and preserved the Jews of Nehemiah's day during this period of stress. But because they chose their own problem-solving method, they sank into the quicksand of increasing compromise.

We know by Nehemiah's reaction to the peoples complaints that he knew these four principles found in the Law:

- It is not wrong to lend money to a non-Jew for interest.

- It is not wrong to lend money to a Jew.

- It is wrong to demand interest on a loan to a Jew.

- It is wrong to enslave a fellow Jew.

Nehemiah got angry because the people knowingly ignored and disobeyed God's Word. That's a pretty good reason to get angry! Righteous indignation is appropriate. When Gods beautiful pattern is violated, something is wrong if we don't feel uneasy. It's difficult to maintain a sweet spirit when you see individuals misusing their tongues, conducting their lives immorally, or ignoring direct counsel from the Book of books. — Charles R. Swindoll, *Hand Me Another Brick* (Nashville: Thomas Nelson, 1998).

14. Is the practice of charging interest OK today?

The reason for such a stern prohibition against charging interest was that all too many in Israel used this method to avoid helping the poor and their own fellow citizens. Deuteronomy 23:20 did say, "You may charge a foreigner interest." Apparently this was the same as charging interest for a business loan or an investment. The foreigner fell under the category of the "resident alien" who had taken up permanent residence among the Israelites. But where the law protected a "resident alien" with the same privileges granted a native Israelite, we may expect the same prohibitions against loaning at interest to the poor (see Lev 25:35).

Of course, all morality condemned excessive rates of interest. Proverbs 28:8 warned, "He who increases his wealth by exorbitant interest amasses it for another, who will be kind to the poor." The prophet Ezekiel also described the "righteous person" as one who "does not lend at usury or take excessive interest" (Ezek 18:8, see also 18:13, 17; 22:12).

What has changed the sentiment in modern times on legitimate forms of interest-taking is an altered perception of the nature and use of money. In the first place, loans today are mostly needed for quite different purposes. In that day it was only a matter of extreme and dire need that would force a person into the position of needing to borrow. In these cases what was owed to one another was compassion. People were to help one another, not use their neighbor's calamity as the opportunity to realize quick and illegitimate profits.

In modern times loans are required principally as a means of increasing the capital with which one works. Unless one has the increased capital, one may not be capable of bringing in the increased revenue. But in ancient times such concerns were not as large as they have become. Loans then were almost exclusively for the purpose of relieving destitution and extreme poverty.

While Hebrew uses two different terms for interest, it is doubtful one can distinguish between them, such as between a long-term and short-term loan, or an exorbitant rate of interest versus a fair rate of return for the use of one's money. Neither can it be said that one relates to the substance loaned and the other to the method by which the loan was computed.

It is a reasonable conclusion that interest was and is still approved for those ventures not attempting to circumvent one's obligation to the poor. This thesis is reinforced by Jesus' allusion to and apparent approval of taking interest for commercial ventures in Matthew 25:27 and Luke 19:23. — Walter C. Kaiser Jr. et al., *Hard Sayings of the Bible* (Downers Grove, IL: InterVarsity, 1996), 152.

15. Nehemiah is all about building the wall. How much does that show up in this chapter? Circle every occurrence of the word "wall" in this chapter.

At this point, I am indebted to Frank R. Tillapaugh for some important thoughts, based on the fact that in order to have a public meeting Nehemiah must have pulled his workers off the wall. In normal circumstances this would not have been remarkable, but these were not normal circumstances. Nehemiah's one goal was to build the wall and to build it quickly before the effort could be stopped by Israel's enemies. He had everyone working. They were working from the dawn's first light until the stars came out. In fact, from the moment three days after he had arrived in Jerusalem, when he had begun the building, until now, there had been only one small interval in which the work had been stopped, and that was when a hostile armed attack had seemed imminent (Neh. 4:13–14). As soon as the threat passed, Nehemiah had the people back on the walls again.

Yet now Nehemiah stopped the work and held a public meeting. Why was this? Tillapaugh says it was because the situation had changed. There was a problem within now, and it was of such overriding importance that it was necessary to deal with it immediately. "What good was it to build the wall," asked Tillapaugh, "if inside the wall there were people who were exploiting one another?" — James Montgomery Boice, *Nehemiah: An Expositional Commentary* (Grand Rapids, MI: BakerBooks, 2005), 64.

16. Somethings are worth stopping the progress on the wall over. What is the application for us?

We must ask that question again today, and we must ask it of ourselves. What good is it to build great evangelical institutions, constructing walls against the "evil" of our opposing, secular world, if within the walls the so-called people of God are indistinguishable from those without? What good is it to preserve a separate "Christian" identity if Christians behave like unbelievers? To put it in sharp terms, we need to stop calling the world to repent until we repent ourselves. — James Montgomery Boice, *Nehemiah: An Expositional Commentary* (Grand Rapids, MI: BakerBooks, 2005), 64.

17. Verse 13. Nehemiah shook out the folds of his robe. What is the deal with that?

Nehemiah made sure it happened. He called the priests and had the nobles and officials take an oath to do what they had promised. It was the equivalent of drafting a notarized agreement. Then he perf ormed a symbolic act, shaking out his garments as a prophetic warning that God would "shake down" anyone who had promised to do the right thing but then later reneged on it. — James Montgomery Boice, *Nehemiah: An Expositional Commentary* (Grand Rapids, MI: BakerBooks, 2005), 66

18. How does the story end?

The astonishing thing about this chapter is that Nehemiah succeeded. We know that he faced stiff opposition, because the nobles did not respond when he approached them earlier. Nevertheless, after Nehemiah had exposed the wrong being done and had challenged the offenders to return the pledged fields, vineyards, olive groves, and houses, refund the interest, and stop the usury, the nobles responded, "We will give it back ... we will not demand anything more from them. We will do as you say" (v. 12). — James Montgomery Boice, *Nehemiah: An Expositional Commentary* (Grand Rapids, MI: BakerBooks, 2005), 66.

19. What do you want to remember from today's study?

20. How can we pray for one another this week?

Nehemiah: Building a Life of Service

Lesson #5: Prioritize

Nehemiah 6.1 – 3, 15 – 16; 8.1 – 3, 5 - 8

Andy Stanley has a great message on this story. Email your people and invite them to watch it at https://www.youtube.com/watch?v=Dh9BCLdE_Vs

OPEN

Share your name and one thing you find your mind returning to these days.

DIG

1. Overview. Let's read today's assigned reading, looking for application.

Now learn this about the devil: He's very clever. He's come to these people as a roaring lion, and that didn't work. So now, he's coming to these people as an angel of light. Sometimes, Satan comes to terrify us, and sometimes he comes to entice us. And so since the more he tried to terrify these people, the more they worked, the devil thought he'd try something else. So he inspired his henchmen to say to Nehemiah, "Nehemiah, we've come to respect you. We'd like to invite you down to one of the villages, to the plain of Ono. We're going to have a love-in; we're going to have a friendly conference, on neutral ground, down in some beautiful valley."

I've learned this: Beware of the world's friendship—just beware of the world's friendship. This vile world is no friend of grace. And Satan's motives never change. They're right there in verse 2: "They thought to do me mischief" (Nehemiah 6:2). Don't get all excited, if the newspapers say something good about us. The world, per se, is no friend of grace. Now be nice, be courteous, and publish glad tidings, wherever you can; but, don't ever think that this world, no matter how kind they may seem, is a friend of grace. Somewhere there is mischief in the making. And many times, we want to pow-wow and parley with the world.

One of my favorite old stories is of a hunter who was out hunting for a bear one time. He saw a bear in the woods, drew a bead on the bear, and the bear stuck up both paws, and said, "Oh, hold it. Don't pull that trigger. Now be reasonable about that thing. I want to talk with you about this thing." Now the bear said to the hunter, "It seems to me that the reason you're trying to shoot me is you want a fur coat. Is that right?" And the hunter said, "Well, that is right. I want a bear coat, a bear-skin coat." And the bear said, "You know, everybody's got his needs. I've been out here in the woods. I'm just looking for a good meal. I have needs. You have needs. Lay that gun down, and come out here in the middle of road, and let's talk about it." So the hunter laid the gun down. And they went out in the middle of the road to talk about it. And when it was over, the man had a fur coat, and the bear had a good meal. — Adrian Rogers, "Rebuilding the Walls," in *Adrian Rogers Sermon Archive* (Signal Hill, CA: Rogers Family Trust, 2017), Ne 4–6.

2. What do we learn about our enemy the devil from Nehemiah's enemy?

Regardless of the nature of your vision or visions, if you are not careful, you will get distracted. The daily grind of life is hard on visions. Life is now. Bills are now. Crisis is now. Vision is later. It is easy to lose sight of the main thing, to sacrifice the best for the sake of the good. All of us run the risk of allowing secondary issues to rob us of the joy of seeing our visions through to completion. Distractions can slowly kill a vision. — *Visioneering: Your Guide for Discovering and Maintaining Personal Vision*, Andy Stanley

3. What do we learn about defeating our enemy from the way Nehemiah defeated his enemy?

That's exactly what the devil is trying to do right here. And you know what Nehemiah said? "Hey, why should I come down? I am doing a great work."

Does God have a plan for your life? Indeed, He does. Then, find God's plan, whatever it is, stay with it, and don't you get derailed. I had a man ask me the other day, "Have you thought about going into politics?" I told him this: "I had rather be a Baptist preacher than to be the President of the United States." I mean that with all of my heart. I would have to step down to be the President of the United States. Don't forsake your calling. You mothers, you're doing a great job raising your children. And the devil will come to you with a very attractive offer that has a lot of glamour to it, and you'll think, "Boy, I won't have to be a homemaker. I can move up." And you come down off the wall, and you forsake your calling from Almighty God.

Church workers, deacons, and Sunday School teachers—I've seen them—they're doing a great work, and the world comes, and says, "Oh, Mrs. So-and-so, you're so gifted; you're so talented. We want you to be the first vice president of our club, The Society for the Prevention of Cruelty to Grandmothers with Athlete's Foot." And so you say, "Oh, they want me to be the vice president." And you step down off the wall, and give up your Sunday School class. Don't do it. Churches can get sidetracked. We have people who want us to get into this thing, and that thing, and do this, and all of these things. And many of them are good. But I'll tell you what God has called this church to do: to preach the gospel of Jesus Christ till He comes—till He comes. And if the devil cannot get you with derision, if the devil cannot get you with discouragement, if the devil cannot get you with division, if the devil cannot get you with danger, the devil will try to get you with distraction—to get you to come down off the wall. That didn't work, so he keeps on going. He doesn't give up easily, does he? — Adrian Rogers, "Rebuilding the Walls," in *Adrian Rogers Sermon Archive* (Signal Hill, CA: Rogers Family Trust, 2017), Ne 4–6. — *Visioneering: Your Guide for Discovering and Maintaining Personal Vision*, Andy Stanley

4. Nehemiah was invited to a meeting. Sounds innocent enough. What is the problem?

Sanballat and company invited Nehemiah to a meeting. Their plan was to pull him off the project, get him away from his supporters, and then kill him. Nehemiah didn't know the full extent of their plan initially. All he knew was they wanted to have a meeting. For all he knew, they wanted to work out a peace agreement of some kind. It was apparent to everyone in the area that this project was going to be completed. It would make sense that the provinces surrounding Jerusalem would begin normalizing relations with Jerusalem now that they were gaining status in the area. — *Visioneering: Your Guide for Discovering and Maintaining Personal Vision*, Andy Stanley

5. How did Nehemiah know this meeting spelled trouble?

I love his reply: "I am doing a great work and I cannot come down." Now, Mr. or Ms. Reader, I want you to do something a little out of the ordinary. I want you to read that statement again, out loud. Ready? Go. I am doing a great work and I cannot come down. Now read it out loud again. But this time, emphasize the word "great." I am doing a great work and I cannot come down. Nehemiah knew what he was about was a God thing. It was an important thing. He was doing a great work. He didn't have time for a meeting. He would not allow himself to be distracted from his great work. He would stay focused. He was not going to let up. He would be relentless about this thing God had called him to do. Taking time to meet with Sanballat was not a "bad" thing. Making peace with an enemy is normally considered a good idea. But God had called Nehemiah to rebuild the wall. He viewed this opportunity as a distraction. And it is a good thing. Sanballat had no intention of making peace.

6. Read for application. What is the lesson for us?

Every day of your life, every day of my life, opportunities come along that have the potential to distract us from the main things that God has called us to do. Entertainment opportunities, athletic opportunities, financial opportunities, relational opportunities, religious opportunities, investment opportunities, career opportunities, business opportunities, vacation opportunities. The list is endless. In my world, the opportunities with the greatest potential to distract me are almost always good opportunities. Things I can easily justify: planning meetings, counseling, speaking engagements, community functions, conferences. I could be out six nights a week taking advantage of "good" opportunities. Like you, I could be even busier than I already am, making even less progress toward accomplishing the few things I know God has set before me to do. To accomplish the important things you must learn to say no to some good things. More often than not, it is good things that have the greatest potential to distract you from the best things, the vision things. If Nehemiah had accepted Sanballat's invitation, his enemies would have killed him. In the same way there are appointments, hobbies, relationships, and invitations that, if taken advantage of, will kill your chances of accomplishing your vision. — *Visioneering: Your Guide for Discovering and Maintaining Personal Vision*, Andy Stanley

7. **Verse 5. What is the significance of this letter being unsealed?**

In those days, letters were written on papyrus or leather. The custom was to roll the writing material, tie it with a string, and seal it with clay. But this letter was open (v. 5). Sanballat purposefully neglected to seal the letter so as to make its contents known to everyone who handled it. His goal, of course, was to spread the rumor that Nehemiah was trying to establish himself as the king of Judah. Nothing could have been further from the truth. But people usually aren't interested in the truth. If word got out that Nehemiah was laying the groundwork to declare himself king, he would face opposition from all sides. For one thing, his own people were not interested in breaking off ties with the Persian government. For another, if that rumor ever reached the ears of King Artaxerxes, he knew he would find himself back in Susa with a rope around his neck. Either way, Sanballat would be happy. He wanted Nehemiah out of the way. It didn't matter to him who did his dirty work. Nehemiah could have easily justified going on the defensive. A lot was at stake. Kings weren't very patient with governors who allowed their political aspirations to go to their heads. Besides that, the workers in Jerusalem were itching for an excuse to quit. But once again Nehemiah stayed focused on the task at hand. He didn't take time off to defend himself. He wasn't worried about what might be. He continued to work toward what could and should be. — *Visioneering: Your Guide for Discovering and Maintaining Personal Vision*, Andy Stanley

8. Verses 6 – 8. What are Nehemiah's enemies up to here?

Shemaiah, a Jew living in Jerusalem, invited Nehemiah to his house for a meeting. When Nehemiah arrived, Shemaiah fabricated a story about a plot on Nehemiah's life. According to the story, Sanballat was planning to send an assassin into the city to murder Nehemiah in his sleep. Nehemiah's only hope, according to Shemaiah, was to run to the temple and cling to the altar. This was a pretty ingenious plot. You see, only priests were allowed into the area of the temple that housed the altar. Nehemiah was not a priest. To violate the temple in this way would discredit him among the Jews. There was an exception to this rule. According to the Law, there were certain circumstances in which a person other than a priest could go into the temple for refuge. If someone accidentally killed another person and the victim had a relative who was likely to take revenge, he was allowed to enter the temple and cling to the altar for refuge. The assailant would be safe there until a judge could hear the case (Numbers 35:6–15). So there were opportunities for people to go into the temple for asylum. But this clearly was not one of those occasions. Shemaiah was trying to trick Nehemiah into making a decision that would discredit him in front of all the people in Israel. To run to the temple for refuge would not only be a violation of the Law, it would undermine his authority as a leader. Word would get out that the governor was hiding in the temple from a would-be assassin. That wouldn't exactly instill confidence in the workers. Not to mention the fact that there was no assassin. — *Visioneering: Your Guide for Discovering and Maintaining Personal Vision*, Andy Stanley

9. What do we learn from Nehemiah's example in verse 11?

Once again, Nehemiah refused to be distracted from the work. His response tells us something about how he viewed himself in relation to his vision. But I said, "Should a man like me flee? And could one such as I go into the temple to save his life? I will not go in." (v. 11) Had Nehemiah been in this thing simply for his own interest, he would have had every reason to run. But Nehemiah had not only embraced this vision, the vision had embraced him. Compared to the great work to which he had been called, the threat of assassination seemed trivial. This was another way of saying, "I am doing a great work. I cannot come down even to protect my life. There is something bigger at stake than my safety." Nehemiah understood the magnitude and significance of his vision. "Should a man like me, a man who has been given this sacred responsibility—this divine assignment—abandon the task to save his own life?" Nehemiah recognized he was a part of something bigger than himself. He knew he was expendable. So he refused to run. — *Visioneering: Your Guide for Discovering and Maintaining Personal Vision*, Andy Stanley

10. Back to verse 1. What do we know about the enemies? Start with Sanballat. What do we know about him? Perhaps you have a study Bible with a note.

Who were they? Sanballat's name is Babylonian, and Sanballat is referred to elsewhere (Neh. 2:10, 19; 13:28) as a "Horonite"—that is, a native of Beth-Horon, situated eighteen miles northwest of Jerusalem. Nehemiah will tell us in chapter 13 that Sanballat's daughter married the son of Eliashib, the high priest (13:28). Historical records inform us that Sanballat was governor of Samaria in 407 B.C., thirty-eight years after Nehemiah came to Jerusalem, and that his two sons bore Jewish names. Informed guesswork suggests that he married a Jew, although he was not Jewish, and that he was an ambitious politician and ruler, eager to please his Persian masters by suggesting intrigue on the part of Nehemiah and his team of builders. The last thing Sanballat needed was trouble at his own back door, and his renewed attack on Nehemiah smacks of political opportunism. — Derek W. H. Thomas, *Ezra & Nehemiah*, ed. Richard D. Phillips, Philip Graham Ryken, and Iain M. Duguid, *Reformed Expository Commentary* (Phillipsburg, NJ: P&R Publishing, 2016), 289.

11. What do we know about Tobiah?

Tobiah is a Jewish name, and like Sanballat, Tobiah has family connections through his son's marriage to the daughter of a high-ranking official in Jerusalem. The issue will become difficult for Nehemiah, since the upper levels of society in the city think of Tobiah as one of them and resent Nehemiah's suspicions toward him (Neh. 6:17–19). It is possible that Tobiah, like Sanballat, is already a governor (in his case, of Ammon), and if not, he soon will be. And like Sanballat, he is keen to protect his political reputation with his masters by joining in pointing the finger at Nehemiah's supposed anti-Persian ambitions. Tobiah's employment of religious slogans might appear as evidence of a godly heart, but it is nothing of the sort; it is merely a utilitarian device for political ambition and greed. — Derek W. H. Thomas, *Ezra & Nehemiah*, ed. Richard D. Phillips, Philip Graham Ryken, and Iain M. Duguid, *Reformed Expository Commentary* (Phillipsburg, NJ: P&R Publishing, 2016), 289.

12. Lastly, Geshem. What do we know about him?

Geshem the Arab is, in the opinion of many commentators, the most powerful of the three. He and his son rule a hegemony of Arabian tribes that had taken over Edom and Moab (Judah's neighbors to the east and south) in addition to territories to the southwest, en route to Egypt. Geshem, Sanballat, and Tobiah form an unholy trinity of opposition against the triune God of Israel. The age-old conflict between the offspring of the woman and the offspring of the serpent is gaining momentum (cf. Gen. 3:15).

The alliance of these three power brokers may seem a unified attempt, but their allegiance is merely negative: all three need to ensure that Jerusalem does not rise in political power, and the best way to prevent this is by a political alliance. Once Jerusalem is out of the way, however, their personal ambitions would ensure that they promoted their own interests. It is a common enough phenomenon that those who have nothing in common will ally themselves against another who poses a threat to their individual ambitions. Nowhere is this seen with greater clarity and deadly import than in the alliance of Jewish leaders and Roman authorities in the crucifixion of Christ. — Derek W. H. Thomas, *Ezra & Nehemiah*, ed. Richard D. Phillips, Philip Graham Ryken, and Iain M. Duguid, *Reformed Expository Commentary* (Phillipsburg, NJ: P&R Publishing, 2016), 290.

13. How are these enemies feeling at the beginning of Nehemiah 6?

From the vantage point of Nehemiah's enemies (Neh. 6:1), the completion of the wall is a threat. Their goal to prevent Jerusalem from becoming a fortified city is crumbling as each stone is set in place and each breach filled. Apart from hanging the great doors, the task is well on the way to completion. Time is short, and any attempt to prevent further construction through military intervention or hindering of supplies seems futile. The only way open is to attack Nehemiah's character and sow the seeds of distrust. — Derek W. H. Thomas, *Ezra & Nehemiah*, ed. Richard D. Phillips, Philip Graham Ryken, and Iain M. Duguid, Reformed Expository Commentary (Phillipsburg, NJ: P&R Publishing, 2016), 290.

14. What is Nehemiah feeling at this stage in the story?

The last lap in any race—literal or metaphorical—is often the most challenging. All of us can recall people who quit even when the finish line was in sight. Nehemiah's enemies come on the scene in chapter 6 with one final, last-ditch effort to discourage his strong finish. Yet Nehemiah asked two questions that helped fuel his successful finish. When he was tempted to get off on side streets, he kept focused: "Why should the work cease while I leave it and go down to you?" (v. 3). And when tempted to get on the sidelines, he kept faithful and asked, "Should such a man as I flee?" (v. 11). It is not how long our race may be, nor even how difficult the task, but how we finish that is most important.

Nehemiah's goal was finally in sight. The walls were rebuilt, and all that remained was hanging the gates. He was on the last lap of a long race that had carried him over many hills and through many valleys. As he sprinted to the finish line, he shouted to us. Can you hear him? "Stay off the side streets! Keep focused!" and "Stay off the sidelines! Keep faithful!" Finishing our own task is a hallmark of success in life. — O. S. Hawkins, *The Jesus Code* (Nashville: Thomas Nelson, 2014).

15. What do you admire about Nehemiah's enemies in Nehemiah 6.5?

Nehemiah's enemies were nothing if not persistent. Four times they made their request. Four times Nehemiah gave the same response! Was it a sign of their desperation or weakness? We should not so easily dismiss their lack of invention. Deploying repeated temptations has proved a winning strategy for Satan. A battering ram might eventually force a point of weakness to give way. And it is to Nehemiah's credit (some might say stubbornness) that his resolve was so entirely unflinching. If he was correct in his assessment (and from our perspective, of course, he was), he is just the kind of leader you want in charge when an enemy is camped on your doorstep! — Derek W. H. Thomas, *Ezra & Nehemiah*, ed. Richard D. Phillips, Philip Graham Ryken, and Iain M. Duguid, *Reformed Expository Commentary* (Phillipsburg, NJ: P&R Publishing, 2016), 292.

16. What do you admire about Nehemiah?

Sanballat—Nehemiah's longtime nemesis—and his deceitful friends made a final attempt to derail him. They sought to trick him into a meeting that was designed to get him off on a side street. "Come, let us meet . . . in the plain of Ono" (Nehemia 6:2) was their invitation. Fortunately, a focused Nehemiah said no: "I am doing a great work, so that I cannot come down" (v. 3).

So often, when our own task is almost done, some Sanballat comes along, seemingly harmless, to get us to lose focus. What is Ono? It is nothing more than a side street. We have all gotten off on them at one time or another. I often did that literally during the fifteen years my family and I lived in Fort Lauderdale. It is called the "Venice of America" because there are more than two hundred miles of waterways within its city limits. There are thousands of homes on the canals that wind their way through the city, so water taxis are a popular mode of transportation. Those who live there and drive cars learn quickly that if you want to get anywhere, you stay on the main roads. Each time I tried to beat the traffic by taking a side street, I would end up on a cul-de-sac, a circle, or worse, a dead end into a canal. Ono may appear to be a good thing, but in this case the good is the enemy of the best.

So what can keep us off the side streets when we are so near a finish line? Focus—and Nehemiah had a laser-like focus: "I am doing a great work, so that I cannot come down. Why should the work cease while I leave it and go down to you?" (v. 3). Stay off the side streets! Keep focused! — O. S. Hawkins, *The Jesus Code* (Nashville: Thomas Nelson, 2014).

17. Matthew 13.22 is a good cross-reference. What kept this third soil from bearing fruit?

This is the person who makes a real heart decision to receive God's Word and begins to grow in relationship with Him. However, God's Word doesn't have first place in their life and their heart is divided. They become preoccupied with distractions such as anxieties, the desire for more material possessions, work and daily activities or recreational pursuits. These distractions begin to take over their life and crowd out the voice of God's Spirit. — Ché Ahn and Bill Johnson, *Grace of Giving, the: Unleashing the Power of a Generous Heart* (Grand Rapids, MI: Chosen, 2013).

18. Philippians 3.13 – 14 is another good cross-reference. What was the key to Paul's success?

An athlete running a race must fix his eyes on something ahead of himself. He can't watch his feet or he'll fall on his face. He can't be distracted by the other runners. He must focus on the goal straight ahead.

Paul's remarkable concentration was the result of two things. First, he chose to forget "those things which are behind." That includes boths good and bad things. It means we should not dwell on past virtuous deeds and achievements any more than we should think about past sins and failures. Unfortunately, many Christians are so distracted by the past that they don't make any current progress.

Instead of looking at the past, Paul focused on the future. "Reaching forward" pictures a runner stretching every muscle to reach the goal. To do that he has to eliminate the distractions and concentrate only on the goal ahead. Do you have that kind of concentration in your desire to become like Christ? — John MacArthur, *Truth for Today : A Daily Touch of God's Grace* (Nashville, Tenn.: J. Countryman, 2001), 148.

19. What do you want to remember and apply from today's study?

20. How can we pray for each other this week?

Nehemiah: Building a Life of Service

Lesson #6: Praise

Nehemiah 8.9 – 12; 12.27 - 31

OPEN

Share your name and one thing that is sure to put a smile on your face.

DIG

1. Nehemiah 6.15 recalls the completion of the wall. What is the rest of Nehemiah about?

Nehemiah wanted to rebuild the wall, but beyond that objective he had the far more significant objective of rebuilding the nation. — James Montgomery Boice, *Nehemiah: An Expositional Commentary* (Grand Rapids, MI: BakerBooks, 2005), 89.

2. Look at the first 8 verses of Nehemiah 8. What is happening in this chapter?

The construction of the city wall complete, all the people had gathered in the city for an entire morning of Scripture reading and exposition. Ezra and thirteen other men stood on a custom-built wooden platform while thirteen other Levites and instructors moved among the crowd, providing explanations of what they were hearing. While Ezra and his team read from the Book of the Law (the first five books of the Old Testament), the Levites "gave the sense," translating the Hebrew text into Aramaic and probably providing a running commentary (Neh. 8:8). The effect on the people was nothing short of overwhelming: "all the people wept as they heard the words of the Law" (v. 9). Faithful, passionate exposition of Scripture is one of God's best gifts to us. — Derek W. H. Thomas, *Ezra & Nehemiah*, ed. Richard D. Phillips, Philip Graham Ryken, and Iain M. Duguid, *Reformed Expository Commentary* (Phillipsburg, NJ: P&R Publishing, 2016), 334.

3. Nehemiah 8.9 – 12. What do we learn about Christian living from this passage?

"Man's chief end," the Westminster divines insist, "is to glorify God and enjoy him forever." Joy was God's plan from the very beginning. Nowhere is this spelled out more clearly than in the account of the creation of Adam and Eve. They enjoyed face-to-face fellowship with God and the delights of a pleasure garden as he walked with them in the cool of the day (Gen. 3:8). And this is what the psalmist evidently thought when he referred to God as "my exceeding joy" (Ps. 43:4). This joy of fellowship with God accompanied by contentment and integration in the environment in which God has placed us has been destroyed by the entrance of sin into the world. Joy, however, is what redemption ultimately restores—though the experience of it here and now is often intermittent. One of the most thrilling and unexpected actions of our Lord is that on the verge of his betrayal and crucifixion, his concern was for our joy. Yes, our joy is seen as the goal of his redemptive work on our behalf: "But now I am coming to you, and these things I speak in the world, that they may have my joy fulfilled in themselves" (John 17:13). — Derek W. H. Thomas, *Ezra & Nehemiah,* ed. Richard D. Phillips, Philip Graham Ryken, and Iain M. Duguid, *Reformed Expository*

Commentary (Phillipsburg, NJ: P&R Publishing, 2016), 333.

4. The people had been reading from the Book of the Law—the Pentateuch. Any hint as to what they might have been reading?

Apparently part of what Ezra and his associates read to the people, or at least to the leaders, included Leviticus 23 (v. 13). In Leviticus 23, God called on the Jews to observe the Feast of Tabernacles (Booths) on the fifteenth through the twenty-first days of the seventh month (Lev. 23:34–36). This was a happy celebration that looked back to the Israelites' years of wandering in the wilderness when they lived in booths that they made out of branches. It also looked forward to their entrance into and permanent residence in the Promised Land. Consequently it would have had special significance for the returned exiles who now again had entered into the Promised Land after being absent from it for years. They had come through a kind of wilderness experience themselves. They even had to travel through a literal wilderness to get back to their land. — Tom Constable, *Tom Constable's Expository Notes on the Bible* (Galaxie Software, 2003), Ne 8:13.

5. What is all the crying about?

Corporate conviction of sin—a deep awareness of and sensitivity to sin, both generally and specifically—is a mark of revival. As the law was read and explained to the people, it was as if God himself was speaking to them and reading their hearts. They saw themselves as sinners, lawbreakers, more concerned with self than pleasing God. Guilt—not just the feeling of guilt, but a realization that sin rendered them liable to God's just punishment—now overtook them. And they began to weep. They wept collectively with sobs of contrition and a sense of unworthiness. — Derek W. H. Thomas, *Ezra & Nehemiah,* ed. Richard D. Phillips, Philip Graham Ryken, and Iain M. Duguid, *Reformed Expository Commentary* (Phillipsburg, NJ: P&R Publishing, 2016), 334.

6. What do we learn about Christian living from their example of weeping?

But conviction of sin is a means, not an end; the Spirit of God convinces of sin in order to induce repentance, and one of the more striking features of revival movements is the depth of repentance into which both saints and sinners are led. Repentance involves turning away from sin and toward God. Peter's listeners on the day of Pentecost were "cut to the heart," leading the Jerusalem congregation to cry out, "Brothers, what shall we do?" (Acts 2:37). Peter showed them the way of faith, repentance, and discipleship through Jesus Christ, and three thousand of them took Peter's words to heart (vv. 37–41).

> My sins, my sins, my Savior!
> They take such hold on me,
> I am not able to look up,
> Save only, Christ, to Thee.

Do you know anything of this? Have you ever experienced Scripture's searching, exposing work, rendering you almost naked before the face of God? There is no true experience of grace without this unmasking of our sin by the Spirit. — Derek W. H. Thomas, *Ezra & Nehemiah*, ed. Richard D. Phillips, Philip Graham Ryken, and Iain M. Duguid, *Reformed Expository Commentary* (Phillipsburg, NJ: P&R Publishing, 2016), 335.

7. How did Nehemiah respond to their weeping? Again, what is the lesson for us?

Amid the sound of weeping, Nehemiah intervened to insist that it was not a day for weeping but a day for rejoicing (Neh. 8:10). It was a time to celebrate with good food and sweet wine (v. 12). The Levites further ordered the people to be calm and "quiet" (v. 11). It looked as though the people had burst into something of a collective hysteria at the sound of one another's weeping. Such hysteria was inappropriate, for it spoke more of uncertainty than of the assurance of God's forgiveness.

Nehemiah was not suggesting that there is no place for weeping in true expressions of biblical faith, but simply that today is to be a day filled with joy. "Joy," wrote C. S. Lewis, "is the serious business of heaven." Paul rounds off his monumental epistle to the Romans by insisting that the kingdom of God is principally about "righteousness and peace and joy in the Holy Spirit" (Rom. 14:17). Joyless religion fosters and demonstrates unbelief—something that Nehemiah, Paul, and Lewis knew well. — Derek W. H. Thomas, *Ezra & Nehemiah*, ed. Richard D. Phillips, Philip Graham Ryken, and Iain M. Duguid, *Reformed Expository Commentary* (Phillipsburg, NJ: P&R Publishing, 2016), 335–336.

8. What do we learn about Christian holiness from this passage?

Holiness and joy fit together hand in glove for Nehemiah and Ezra, and as Derek Kidner notes, this "should go without saying." The exhortation to rejoice initially seems at odds with the fact that we are told three times in as many verses that the day was "holy" (Neh. 8:9, 10, 11). The day was holy because it was the first day of the seventh month (7:73), and the start of a series of festivals in the Jewish religious calendar, including the Day of Atonement and the Feast of Booths/Tabernacles (Lev. 23:24–25, 27, 34). The first day of the month was a day of "solemn rest" comparable to a Sabbath (v. 24). But the day anticipated the Feast of Booths/Tabernacles—an especially exciting festival for children, who must have enjoyed the prospect of camping, sleeping under temporary shelters in memory of the protection afforded their ancestors during their wilderness wanderings. It does appear as though this feast had been forgotten after being celebrated when the people first returned to the land in Ezra 3, almost a century earlier. — Derek W. H. Thomas, *Ezra & Nehemiah, ed.* Richard D. Phillips, Philip Graham Ryken, and Iain M. Duguid*, Reformed Expository Commentary* (Phillipsburg, NJ: P&R Publishing, 2016), 336.

9. What do we learn about joy from this passage?

We are missing the mark about Christian victory and the life of joy in our Savior. We ought to be standing straight and praising our God!

I must agree with the psalmist that the joy of the Lord is the strength of His people. I do believe that the sad world is attracted to spiritual sunshine—the genuine thing, that is.

Some churches train their greeters and ushers to smile, showing as many teeth as possible. But I can sense that kind of display, and when I am greeted by a person who is smiling because he or she has been trained to smile, I know I am shaking the flipper of a trained seal. When the warmth and joy of the Holy Spirit are in a congregation, however, and the folks are spontaneously joyful, the result is a wonderful influence upon others.

I have said it a hundred times: The reason we have to search for so many things to cheer us up is the fact that we are not really joyful and contentedly happy within.... But we are Christians, and Christians have every right to be the happiest people in the world. — A. W. Tozer, *Tozer for the Christian Leader* (Chicago: Moody Publishers, 2015).

10. What is the difference between happiness and joy?

A HUNDRED YEARS AGO, every Christian knew the meaning of joy. Today, if you ask a group of Christians, "What does joy mean?" most will grope for words, with only one emphatic response: that joy is different from happiness. It's supposedly superior —deep rather than superficial, holy rather than sinful. It's often said to be unemotional, in contrast to that unspiritual thing called happiness. (This also sends the message that anything emotional is bad.)

Saying that joy isn't about being happy is like saying that rain isn't wet or ice isn't cold. Scripture, church history, dictionaries, and common language simply don't support this conclusion.

I googled "define joy," and the first result was this dictionary definition: "a feeling of great pleasure and happiness." This definition harmonizes with other dictionaries and ordinary conversations, yet it contradicts countless Christian books and sermons that claim joy and happiness are radically different.

The church's misguided distinction between joy and happiness has twisted the words. A Christian psychiatrist says, "Happiness is secular, joy sacred."[1] So we should be joyful but not happy when reading the Bible, praying, and worshiping? Is the Christian life really divided into the secular and sacred, or is every part of our lives, even the ordinary moments, to be centered in God?

God created not only our minds but also our hearts. Sure, emotions can be manipulated, but so can minds. God designed us to have emotions, and he doesn't want us to shun or disregard them. It's ill advised to redefine joy and happiness and pit them against each other rather than embracing the emotional satisfaction of knowing, loving, and following Jesus.

I've become so accustomed to reading misstatements by contemporary Christians about joy and happiness that when I read a devotional by Joni Eareckson Tada I cheered aloud at her words. Tada opens by citing Psalm 68:3: "May the righteous be glad and rejoice before God; may they be happy and joyful" (NIV). She then writes:

> We're often taught to be careful of the difference between joy and happiness. Happiness, it is said, is an emotion that depends upon what "happens." Joy by contrast, is supposed to be enduring, stemming deep from within our soul and which is not affected by the circumstances surrounding us. . . . I don't think God had any such hair-splitting in mind. Scripture uses the terms interchangeably along with words like delight, gladness, blessed. There is no scale of relative spiritual values applied to any of these. Happiness is not relegated to fleshly-minded sinners nor joy to heaven-bound saints.[2]

Joni Eareckson Tada is absolutely right. Modern distinctions between happiness and joy are completely counterintuitive. This is no minor semantic issue. For too long we've distanced the gospel from what Augustine, Aquinas, Pascal, the Puritans, Wesley, Moody, and many other spiritual visionaries said God created us to desire —and what he desires for us —happiness.

Do we seriously want to take issue with Charles Spurgeon (1834–1892) when he said, "My dear Brothers and Sisters, if anybody in the world ought to be happy, we are the people. . . . How boundless our privileges! How brilliant our hopes!"[3] Was he wrong to say we ought to be happy, and would his meaning be more spiritual if he'd said "joyful" instead? To declare joy sacred and happiness secular closes the door to dialogue with unbelievers. — Randy Alcorn, *60 Days of Happiness: Discover God's Promise of Relentless Joy* (Carol Stream, IL: Tyndale, 2017).

11. Tozer said, "But we are Christians, and Christians have every right to be the happiest people in the world." Do you agree?

Maximizing our joy in God is what we were created for. "But wait a minute," someone says, "what about the glory of God? Didn't God create us for His glory? But here you are saying that He created us to pursue our joy!" Which is it? Are we created for His glory or our joy?

Oh how passionately I agree that God created us for His glory! Yes! Yes! God is the most God-centered person in the universe. This is the heartbeat of everything I preach and write. This is what Christian Hedonism is designed to preserve and pursue! God's chief end is to glorify God. This is written all over the Bible. It is the aim of all God does.

God's goal at every stage of creation and salvation is to magnify His glory. You can magnify with a microscope or with a telescope. A microscope magnifies by making tiny things look bigger than they are. A telescope magnifies by making gigantic things (like stars), which look tiny, appear more as they really are. God created the universe to magnify His glory the way a telescope magnifies stars. Everything He does in our salvation is designed to magnify the glory of His grace like this. — John Piper, *The Dangerous Duty of Delight* (Sisters, OR: Multnomah Publishers, 2001), 16–17.

12. Lewis said, "It is a Christian's duty, as you know, to be as happy as you can be." Do you agree?

So if Christian Hedonism is old-fashioned, why is it so controversial? One reason is that it insists that joy is not just the spin-off of obedience to God, but part of obedience. It seems as though people are willing to let joy be a by-product of our relationship to God, but not an essential part of it. People are uncomfortable saying that we are duty-bound to pursue joy.

They say things like, "Don't pursue joy; pursue obedience." But Christian Hedonism responds, "That's like saying, 'Don't eat apples; eat fruit.'" Because joy is an act of obedience. We are commanded to rejoice in God. If obedience is doing what God commands, then joy is not merely the spin-off of obedience, it is obedience. The Bible tells us over and over to pursue joy: "Be glad in the LORD and rejoice, you righteous ones; and shout for joy, all you who are upright in heart" (Psalm 32:11). "Let the nations be glad and sing for joy" (Psalm 67:4). "Delight yourself in the LORD" (Psalm 37:4). "Rejoice that your names are recorded in heaven" (Luke 10:20). "Rejoice in the Lord always; again I will say, rejoice!" (Philippians 4:4).

The Bible does not teach that we should treat delight as a mere by-product of duty. C. S. Lewis got it right when he wrote to a friend, "It is a Christian duty, as you know, for everyone to be as happy as he can." Yes, that is risky and controversial. But it is strictly true. Maximum happiness, both qualitatively and quantitatively, is precisely what we are duty-bound to pursue. — John Piper, *The Dangerous Duty of Delight* (Sisters, OR: Multnomah Publishers, 2001), 13–14.

13. Why is it important that we be as happy as we can be?

Now, you know, that's our best advertisement, is the joy of the Lord. King David loved God with all of his heart, but he lost his joy, and he prayed this in Psalm 51:12: "Restore unto me the joy of thy salvation." He hadn't lost his salvation, but he lost his joy. "Restore unto me the joy of thy salvation, and uphold me with thy free spirit. And then—listen to it—and then will I teach transgressors thy ways, and sinners shall be converted unto thee."

Now, if you're not a joyful Christian, you're not an effective soul winner. You're going around with a Bible under one arm and a tombstone under the other, and saying, "Don't you want to be like I am?" He said, "No, thank you. I've got enough troubles already." No! Listen. It is so essential in winning the lost. — Adrian Rogers, "How to Have Fullness of Joy," in *Adrian Rogers Sermon Archive* (Signal Hill, CA: Rogers Family Trust, 2017), Jn 15:11.

14. Adrian Rogers said a joyless Christian is a contradiction in terms. Do you agree?

A woman lost her house keys. She looked and looked and looked and looked and looked. You've done something like that, haven't you? Just looked everywhere. And then she opened her purse, and there they were. Now, you want me to tell you why she found her keys in her purse? Because that's where she left them, right? Number two: Do you know why she didn't find her keys in the other place? They weren't there. Now, do you know why some folks don't find joy? They're looking for it in the wrong place. They're trying to find it, but you'll never find it, until you look in the right place.

Now, I guess the key verse on joy in all of the Bible is John chapter 15 and verse 11. Look at it. Jesus said, "These things have I spoken unto you, that my joy might remain in you, and that your joy might be full"—"... that my joy might remain in you, that your joy would be full."

The life of a Christian is to be a life of joy. A joyless Christian is a contradiction in terms. It would be like saying a heavenly devil—a joyless Christian. If you don't have joy, there is something wrong. Your life is to be a life of joy—continual joy, conspicuous joy, contagious joy is to be yours, if you know the Lord Jesus Christ. Now, you can know Jesus and not have this joy. That's the reason Jesus is telling us what He's telling us. Joy is not inevitable. It's optional. But you ought to have joy, if you want joy. — Adrian Rogers, "How to Find Joy," in *Adrian Rogers Sermon Archive* (Signal Hill, CA: Rogers Family Trust, 2017), Jn 15:11.

15. Let's walk around this diamond of truth. First, let me ask this. How are our thoughts and our joy related?

To experience maximum joy, you must first improve the quality of your thinking. That was the emphasis of earlier chapters. You are where you are at this point in your life because of the dominating thoughts you have allowed to occupy your mind. Your health, your marriage, your career, and all the other aspects of your life are colored by the quality of your mental diet. These habitual thought patterns, accumulated over a lifetime, trigger your actions and determine your quality of life, even though you are not consciously aware of most of them. As we've discussed, we can train ourselves to be more deliberate about our thoughts. But another way to minimize negative thought patterns is to purposely remove ourselves from negative situations. In this section, you will be encouraged and equipped to become intentional and purposeful with your exposures.

What you let in your heart shapes what you believe, expect, and do.

Sometimes your thoughts are triggered by your surroundings. Sometimes they are triggered by your memory, and other times they are brought about through your imagination. In some cases, a particular thought just seems to come out of nowhere. So if you are to keep your mind on godly things—if you are to dwell on what is lovely, pure, gracious, and just—then it is critical that you have a plan. Choosing to wing it is the same as choosing to fall short of your full potential. Why in the world would you want to do that?

In Philippians, Paul lays out a clear game plan for what we should think about. It is a challenge, but if you and I could not accomplish it, he would not have suggested it. If you believe that your thinking is important and you accept Paul's advice, what is the next step? How do you get to the place where living the 4:8 Principle becomes second nature? You are engineered for joy and delight, but it's easy to unknowingly program yourself for stagnation and mediocrity. Because most of your thinking comes from your exposures, it is easy to become overly influenced by your surroundings. That's why it's so important to protect yourself. — Tommy Newberry, *The 4:8 Principle: The Secret to a Joy-Filled Life* (Carol Stream, IL: Tyndale, 2010).

16. How common is this theme? How important is our joy to God?

YOU MAY BE UNACCUSTOMED TO thinking that God commands us to be happy or to do things that make us happy. But he does. And I'd wager that since the outcome of our obedience would be our happiness, these are commands we would all want to obey — provided we were thinking clearly.

Some people have an intuitive resistance to the notion that happiness is unbiblical, and rightfully so. A blogger says, "Happiness isn't in the Bible? But what about all the commands to rejoice? What about laughter? Please tell me I'm not supposed to always be heavy-hearted, trudging along and begrudging obedience. I want to be a happy Christian!"[1]

Happiness is a privilege. However, since God repeatedly calls upon us to rejoice, delight, and be glad in him, we have an obligation to actually do so.

This makes sense only if the God we love is happy, if the gospel message we embrace and proclaim is happy, if Heaven is a happy place, and if it makes God happy for us to be happy. It makes sense if we understand that people long to be happy and won't turn to Jesus if they believe there's no happiness in him.

Others will judge whether there's happiness in Jesus by whether they see happiness in his followers. Hence, our happiness is, in multiple respects, a Christian duty.

But what an incredibly wonderful duty it is . . . like being required to eat Mom's apple pie! We're accustomed to thinking of duty as drudgery. Yet we know that the duties of loving a spouse or caring for a child or serving one's country can bring satisfaction, contentment, and happiness.

People have told me it's easy to speak of happiness in a prosperous country, but how dare we say God expects those impoverished and suffering to be joyful? In fact, poor Christians often have joy that radiates far beyond what we typically see in Western churches, and they have much to teach us.

I've studied more than 2,700 Scripture passages where words such as joy, happiness, gladness, merriment, pleasure, celebration, cheer, laughter, delight, jubilation, feasting, exultation, and celebration are used. Throw in the words blessed and blessing, which often connote happiness, and the number increases. — Randy Alcorn, *60 Days of Happiness: Discover God's Promise of Relentless Joy* (Carol Stream, IL: Tyndale, 2017).

17. How can we be joyful when circumstances are difficult?

Surprisingly, many people have this backward; they believe that circumstances cause their thoughts. However, if you are dissatisfied with the conditions of your life, you now know what you need to do: Hold up your circumstances as a mirror and figure out what types of thoughts could be causing the blemishes you spot in the reflection. After all, you would never blame the mirror for what it reflects back to you. Your life today corresponds with your thoughts from the past. Virtually all causation is mental. If you want to produce a specific outcome in your life, you must trace back from that outcome and identify the types of thoughts that would produce such a result. For every effect in your life, there is a thought or crop of thoughts that are responsible.

What you sow in thought, either useful or useless, manifests itself sooner or later in your circumstances. As your coach, I want to encourage you to start living more consistently with a central law of the Bible: Whatever you sow, you shall also reap (see Galatians 6:7). Put another way, "whoever sows sparingly will also reap sparingly, and whoever sows generously will also reap generously" (2 Corinthians 9:6, NIV).

This law works 24/7 everywhere in the world, for sinner and saint alike. Specifically, if you want to reap more joy, you must plant joyful thoughts—and lots of them. It is simply impossible to produce a result that has not first been formed in thought. There's no need to take my word for it. When you look through the all-time best seller, you will have God's word on it. God promises that all your actions produce reactions, that what you sow in thought or deed, you shall certainly reap. Consider Matthew 7:2, "For in the same way you judge others, you will be judged, and with the measure you use, it will be measured to you" (NIV); or Job 4:8, "Those who plow iniquity and sow trouble reap the same" (ESV). In Matthew 12:34, Jesus asks, "How can you who are evil say anything good? For out of the overflow of the heart the mouth speaks" (NIV).

Just because a cause is not readily apparent does not mean there is no cause. Often there is such a time lag between the plane of thought and the visible plane that the connection to causation is blurred. However, you can determine causation by careful study of your thought life. Because your thoughts directly or indirectly produce your circumstances, monitor them closely. — Tommy

Newberry, *The 4:8 Principle: The Secret to a Joy-Filled Life* (Carol Stream, IL: Tyndale, 2010).

18. Randy Alcorn tells of a conversation he had with a woman who thought the Christian life was one of bleakness. Imagine you had such a friend. Imagine they invited you to speak into their life and advise them. What advice would you give them?

I talked with a young woman who viewed the Christian life as one of utter dullness. She knew that following Christ was the right thing to do, but she was certain it would mean sacrificing her happiness.

Unless her view changes dramatically, her spiritual future is bleak. It isn't in our nature to continually say no to what we believe would make us happy —or to say yes to something we think would make us unhappy. (Don't mistake perseverance for choosing unhappiness — the man who faithfully loves his wife suffering from dementia is not choosing unhappiness but rather choosing the happiness of honoring his wife, keeping his vows, maintaining his self-respect, and hearing God's "well done.")

So where did this young woman, who was raised in a fine Christian family and church, acquire such an unbiblical notion? Somehow she, like many of us, missed the point of what God calls the good news of great joy.

Around 150 years ago, Pastor Charles Spurgeon told his church what pastors today should tell theirs: "God made human beings, as He made His other creatures, to be happy. . . . They are in their right element when they are happy."[2]

Celebration and gladness of heart have characterized the church, including the suffering church, throughout history. Scripturally, the culture of God's people is not one of misery, anger, and whining but of joy, happiness, gratitude, eating and drinking, singing and dancing, and making music. It's not the people who know God who have reason to be miserable —it's those who don't.
— Randy Alcorn, *60 Days of Happiness: Discover God's Promise of Relentless Joy* (Carol Stream, IL: Tyndale, 2017).

19. What practical steps can we take to become obedient to the command of God to rejoice in the Lord always?

I HEARD A STORY OF someone who asked a man why he was so happy. The man picked up a binder filled with hundreds of handwritten pages and explained, "Every time someone does something kind for me, I write it in this book. And every time I feel very good about something, I write it in this book."

The questioner said, "I wish I could be as happy as you."

"If you kept a book like this, you would be."

"But the book is so big . . . I haven't had many kind things done for me, and I haven't felt good very often."

"I might have thought that too, if I hadn't recorded them all. I've learned to see and remember and be grateful for kindness and happiness when they come. Try it. Every time you doubt, read your entries and you'll see all you have to be grateful for." — Randy Alcorn, *60 Days of Happiness: Discover God's Promise of Relentless Joy* (Carol Stream, IL: Tyndale, 2017).

20. What do you want to recall from today's study?

21. How can we pray for each other this week?

Made in the USA
Las Vegas, NV
03 October 2021

31645124R00055